Lund and Learning

Carl Fehrman

Lund and Learning

An informal history of Lund University

Translated by Alan Crozier

Lund University Press

The cover picture shows the oldest university building situated in Lundagård, completed in 1584 by master builder Didrik.

Lund University Press
Box 141
S-221 00 Lund
Sweden
ISBN 91-7966-008-8
Art nr 20021

Chartwell-Bratt Ltd
Old Orchard Road
Bromley, Kent BR1 2NE
England
ISBN 0-86238-133-9

Cover: Harry Kumlien
Printed in Sweden
Studentlitteratur
Lund 1987

Contents

Preface

This is a translation of *Lärdomens Lund*, a book first published by Liber Förlag in 1984 and reprinted in 1985. The text has been abridged and partly rewritten for the English edition: some material of exclusively local interest has been eliminated; on the other hand, greater space has been devoted to the network of contacts with foreign universities and personal contacts with foreign scholars.

A history of a university, however concise it may be, should attempt to illuminate a number of widely varying spheres and contexts. It must consider not only intellectual history and the history of science but also general history and topography; it must treat individual persons of historical importance, while at the same time shedding light on what is now called the history of mentalities.

The aim of the book is to tell in an informal way of people and places, of important epochs and significant episodes in Lundensian scholarship from the Middle Ages to the present day. There are larger and more scientific historical presentations of Lund University, in particular the four Swedish-language volumes of *Lunds Universitets Historia* which were published in conjunction with the tricentennial celebration of the university in 1968. Naturally, a great deal of the material here has been derived from this and older works; the bibliography in the Swedish version of *Lärdomens Lund* may be consulted for full details.

For the decades since the 1930s the author has been able to apply the somewhat disputed method known as participant observation. As a native of Lund, a student here in the 1930s, as lecturer in the arts faculty since 1945, as professor of literature and poetics between 1958 and 1980, and since then in my emeritus years, I have participated in university life on various levels; during this time I could not have failed to make a few personal observations, reflections, and comparisons.

The task of writing this popular history of Lund University was initially assigned to me by members of the governing body of the university, among them the present University Chancellor, Carl-Gustaf Andrén; the translation has likewise come about on the initiative of the university. The appearance of the book in its present form has been made possible thanks to a grant from the

Crafoord Foundation in Lund. For the preparation of the text the author has benefited greatly from discussions with university colleagues, including my friend Claes Schaar, professor of English, as well as with the translator of the book, Dr Alan Crozier, equally well acquainted with his own university, Cambridge, as with the university milieu of Lund.

CARL FEHRMAN

Lund
January 1987

Introduction
Prologue in Denmark

In the beginning was the cathedral.

If the cathedral represents the spiritual power, a royal mint can be seen as a symbol of the material base.

The mint was founded in the market town of Lund a few years into the eleventh century by Canute the Great, king of England and Denmark. In Adam of Bremen's eleventh-century history of the archbishops of Hamburg, with its wealth of important evidence for the medieval history of Scandinavia, there is a marginal note which names Canute the Great as the founder of Lund. Scania, the modern Skåne, then a Danish province, is mentioned, with its capital the town of *Lundona*, 'which England's conqueror Canute decreed would imitate (or rival) the British London.' History has not fulfilled the king's hopes; every passing century has intensified the difference between the two towns.

Lund is the Swedish word for a grove, and the place-name may denote a pagan cult site. The name of Lund has no linguistic connection with that of London, but the popular belief that the former was named after the latter is of considerable antiquity. The various names of the town shown on the oldest medieval coins which have been dug from the earth in Lund have exactly the same forms as those used for medieval London. Occasionally the mint-master — an Englishman — has added a *D* or *Denemac* (i.e., Denmark) to indicate which of the two towns the coin came from. The similarity in the names of the towns persisted as long as Latin was written or spoken. *Londini Scanorum* or *Lundini Scanorum* can still be read on the title-pages of the oldest publications of the university, from the second half of the seventeenth century.

The cathedral was built towards the end of the eleventh century under the patronage of the Danish king known since his canonization as Canute the Holy. An early copy of his charter, signed 21st May, 1085, records the king's donation of lands and their yields intended to be the economic foundation of the cathedral and the diocese.

In Canute's charter the cathedral is described as 'not yet completed'. At the beginning of the following century the present cathedral was erected on the site of an earlier church. Built of grey sandstone, the cathedral is adorned with magnificent sculptures by foreign masons specially summoned to the town. The vaulted crypt with its rows of columns was dedicated in 1123, and the church

The apse of Lund Cathedral, the best preserved part of the medieval Romanesque cathedral.

itself twenty-two years later. The cathedral on the fertile plain of Lund asserted the importance of the town as an ecclesiastical centre, not just for medieval Denmark but for the whole of Scandinavia for some time to come. From 1104 the archbishop of Lund was primate of all the Nordic countries, a man of considerable temporal and spiritual power. Danish kings were crowned in the cathedral; homage was paid here to Margareta, queen of the united Scandinavian countries.

Late in the eleventh century the cathedral acquired a school — the oldest educational foundation in Scandinavia. Book learning was pursued not only in the cathedral school and the church, but also in the town's monasteries, eight of which had been built in Lund before the middle of the thirteenth century. For higher education the monks went abroad, to the cathedral school in Hildesheim, to the colleges in Prague and Cologne, to the universities in Bologna and Paris. The latter seat of learning saw the establishment in the thirteenth century of a special *Collegium Lundense*.

Like the cathedrals, the cathedral schools, and the guilds, the universities have their origin in the culture of the high Middle Ages. For many centuries they retained something of the hierarchical organization of the monasteries, together with monastic privileges which exempted them from secular authority. Teachers and students were — and have remained — a people apart, with their own emblems, rites, and shrines.

The word university derives from Latin *universitas* 'totality, corporation'. Just as the craftsmen banded together in guilds to protect their rights, the university teachers formed a corporate *universitas magistrorum*, or the teachers and students together formed a community of interests, the *universitas magistrorum et scholarium*. Only later was the the word university understood to mean *universitas scientiarum*, a totality of knowledge and science. Beside the word university, medieval institutes of higher education were often known by the term *studium generale*.

The oldest duty of the universities was to educate clerics, men skilled in the writing of Latin and versed in the law, qualified for the needs of the church and the administration of the towns. Europe's oldest university was founded in Bologna in the twelfth century for the study of jurisprudence; students at the slightly younger university in Paris could read other subjects, chiefly theology and philosophy. The University of Paris was the model for a range of later universities from the thirteenth century on, in France, England, and Germany. The universities in northern Germany in their turn served as models for Scandinavia.

The University of Paris had four faculties, one each for theology, canon law, medicine, and the faculty of philosophy which taught the liberal arts. Students were organized by their country of origin into four 'nations'.

All the medieval archbishops of Lund had received their theological education at foreign seats of learning. Many of them were among the most highly educated men of their times. Archbishop Eskil, who in 1145 consecrated the cathedral in the presence of an illustrious assembly of princes, nobles, and clergy, had studied in Hildesheim; it was there his views on ecclesiastical politics were formed, in particular his conviction that the church should be independent of the state and exempted from paying taxes to the crown. That he maintained his connections with the continent is shown by his close friendship with one of the great men of the French Middle Ages, Saint Bernard, at whose monastery in Clairvaux he spent his last days after retiring from the archbishopric.

Eskil's successor, Absalon, equally renowned in the roles of warrior and churchman, had studied in Paris at the time of the First Crusade. He was in turn succeeded by Andreas Sunesson, who became archbishop in 1201. He was the most learned of the medieval bishops, having studied for over ten years in Paris, Bologna, and Oxford; he had also taught in Paris. He owned a considerable library for his time, which he bequeathed to the cathedral. The thirty manuscript volumes included, apart from the Bible and commentaries, works of Gregory the Great and the scholastic theologian Petrus Lombardus. His knowledge of canon law is evident from his translation of the laws of Scania into Latin, supplemented by explanatory comments. His understanding of the Christian philosophy of the High Middle Ages, and his knowledge of classical history and mythology are documented in his *Hexaëmeron*; this epic poem on the six days of creation, composed in Latin hexameters and intended as a textbook for the priests of the archdiocese, has been called the first popularizing work to come from Lund.

It was to Andreas Sunesson that Saxo Grammaticus dedicated his great history of Denmark, *Gesta Danorum*, which was completed around 1200. Saxo had previously worked as a scribe in Archbishop Absalon's chancery, and had been commissioned by him to write the history. It is written in Classical Latin and modelled directly on the historians of antiquity. The manuscript of *Gesta Danorum* was lost for a time, but it was traced in the sixteenth century by one of the canons of Lund, Christian Pedersen, a humanist and biblical translator well-known for his part in the Danish Reformation. It was through his agency that Saxo's work was printed in Paris in 1514. It soon became famous throughout Europe. The best-known episode in *Gesta Danorum* is the tale of the Danish prince Amletus. The circuitous route from Amletus to Shakespeare's Hamlet thus passed through Lund and Paris.

The archbishop of Lund at the beginning of the fifteenth century was an erudite man who had studied in Paris, Peder Lykke. During his prelacy the Danish king Erik of Pomerania applied to the Pope in 1419 for permission to establish a university in Denmark. Pope Martin V sent a bull to Peder Lykke, authorizing him to found what would have been Scandinavia's first university. It is uncertain whether it would have been established in Copenhagen or Lund, but we know that it was to have only three faculties, for arts, law, and medicine, and no theological faculty. Because of Erik of Pomerania's preoccupations elsewhere, chiefly in a war with the Hanseatic League, no university was founded. It is probable that the University of Rostock, founded one year previously, was considered enough to satisfy the higher educational needs of the time.

At the Franciscan monastery in Lund, however, a *studium generale* was established, following a decision taken by a provincial chapter in Stockholm and ratified at a general chapter of the order held in 1438. It was possible to study there to become a *baccalaureus* 'bachelor', the lowest degree at that time. The Franciscan monastic college appears to have existed for about a century. The seal of the head teacher, *lector principalis*, has survived; it shows him lecturing from his pulpit with a few pupils before him. This is in all probability the oldest pictorial evidence in the educational history of Lund. Of the library of the Franciscan monastery a few manuscripts are preserved, now in the care of the University Library in Lund.

The seal of the lecturer at the Franciscan monastery school, the oldest pictorial evidence in Lund's educational history. The inscription reads: S' lectoris principalis studii lundensis.

15

The centre of this Danish archbishop's seat was the cathedral and the area known as Lundagård, the Court of Lund or *Curia Lundensis*. The latter was the name of the archbishop's residence and was the administrative centre of the archdiocese. It contained dwelling houses, halls, and an apple orchard. The cathedral school appears to have been situated west of the cathedral. South of the cathedral there still stands the *Liberium*, which since the Reformation has housed the cathedral library and archives. The deanery has survived, having been moved within the precincts of Kulturen, the Museum of Cultural History in Lund.

As both a secular and an ecclesiastical centre, Lund had an important role in medieval Denmark. Two factors accounting for the importance of this *metropolis Daniae* were the geographical location of the town in a fertile region where trade routes converged, and the presence of Canute the Great's royal mint. The see of Lund was a large-scale agricultural enterprise; products from church lands fostered trade beyond the boundaries of the country.

The town, however, experienced its vicissitudes. It was harried by fires and devastated by wars. Towards the end of the Middle Ages, the importance of Lund had diminished. By the fourteenth century Lund was overshadowed by Malmö, which was to become the most important commercial centre in the province; the mint was also moved to Malmö. From 1417 Copenhagen was the capital of the kingdom; Lund thus lost its pride of place as *caput regni*.

A few decades later, Lund was also to lose its position as the country's chief seat of learning. King Christian I sought permission from Pope Sixtus IV — the founder of the Sistine Chapel in Rome — to establish in Denmark a university comprising four faculties. The papal foundation charter commissioned Archbishop Jens Brostrup in Lund, a man who had acquired much of his learning at foreign universities, to direct the organization of the new university. It has been assumed — by a Lund historian, it should be noted — that Jens Brostrup had initially considered Lund as the site of the university, but the king, who had the final say in the matter, preferred his capital, Copenhagen. The archbishop gave his assent in October 1478. In June the following year, 1479, King Christian inaugurated the first university at a celebration in Our Lady's Church in Copenhagen. This was a complete university with all four faculties. The organization was patterned on that of the University of Cologne, from where a number of the first professors also came.

Two years before the University of Copenhagen was founded, Sweden had anticipated Denmark: the University of Uppsala was inaugurated in 1477. In the case of Uppsala it was also Pope Sixtus IV who had issued the bull authorizing the foundation of the university. Although the papal bull mentioned four faculties, as for Copenhagen, the universities of this age were in practice more like Catholic spiritual centres with theology and canon law as the most important subjects and the training of priests and monks as their most important task.

Chapter 1
The Grove of Academe
A University in Lund

Lund in the 1580s. Copperplate by Franz Hogenberg in Liber quartus urbium praecipuarum totius mundi.

The early sixteenth century was a decisive period in the history of Scandinavia, politically, ecclesiastically, and culturally. Lutheranism became the state religion of both Denmark and Sweden.

The Reformation meant the end of Lund's role as archbishop's seat and Catholic centre of learning. A diet held in Copenhagen in 1536 resolved to depose all of Denmark's Catholic bishops. Their property and lands were confiscated by the crown. The era of the mighty princes of the church was over. The state had defeated the church in a power struggle which had been going on throughout the later Middle Ages.

The brick houses in Lundagård which had been the archbishop's residence fell into decay. In their stead the master builder Didrik designed a gabled house adorned with towers, which was intended as a residence for the king's sheriff and for the king himself during his visits to Scania. The house, which was completed in 1584, is the brick building which still stands in Lundagård; it is known today as Lundagårdshuset or *Kungshuset* 'King's House'. A century later, when Danish kings no longer ruled over Scania, it was to become the main building of the Royal University of Lund.

The former cathedral, restored after a fashion by Adam van Düren, became the parish church for the entire town. The Catholic monasteries, of which there had once been twenty-seven in the medieval archbishop's town, were demolished. But the cathedral chapter and school survived. The new evangelical Lutheran doctrine also needed its ministers of the gospel; after study at the cathedral school they could continue at Copenhagen University, now transformed into a Protestant college, or go to Luther's and Melanchthon's university in Wittenberg. In 1619 King Christian IV of Denmark established a grammar school in Lund. Of its five teachers — styled professors — one taught theology, one Latin oratory, one Greek and Hebrew, one logic, and one physics and mathematics.

In the course of the seventeenth century the balance of power in Scandinavia shifted. A war between Denmark and Sweden in the middle of the century ended with the peace of Roskilde in 1658. Part of the settlement was the Danish cession of Scania to Sweden. This, the beginning of the Swedish epoch in the history of Scania and of Lund, was one of the very few military occupations in Europe that have been to any extent successful up to the present day.

As a step in the incorporation of the Danish provinces into Sweden, Karl X Gustav (Charles X) intended to locate a clerical training college in Scania, the idea being to discourage young men from choosing to pursue their studies in nearby Copenhagen. A plan for how the proposed university was to be organized was drawn up by Bishop Peder Winstrup of Lund, who had studied in Copenhagen as well as in a number of German universities, Wittenberg, Leipzig, and Jena. He himself was a learned Protestant theologian, the author of a three-thousand-page commentary on the Gospel of Matthew. He was the owner of an impressive library and had his own printing press.

The king's plans for the Swedification of the conquered provinces had to be postponed because of his second war against Denmark. Discussion of the planned university in Lund was interrupted by the death of Karl X Gustav. Instead it was the regency government which took power after the king's death which, on the instigation of the Scanian clergy, took the final decision to establish a university in Lund. A key role in this was played by Magnus Gabriel de la Gardie, the most powerful man in the regency. His broad outlook on culture and education from a European point of view was combined with a well-developed network of personal contacts on the continent. He was chancellor of Uppsala University and undeniably the foremost patron of the arts in seventeenth-century Sweden. Viewed in a broader perspective, the foundation of the University of Lund in 1668 can be seen not only as one stage in the Europeanization of Sweden, but also as a part of a great European civilizing process. On 19th December, 1666, the regency issued the four documents which created the new university in Lund: the deed of foundation, the donation charter, the letter of privilege, and the constitution.

Lund was to be the fifth university in the Kingdom of Sweden as it was then, after Uppsala, Dorpat (Tartu in Estonia), Åbo (Turku in Finland), and Greifswald in Pomerania. The deed of foundation decreed the name of the new university: in memory of Karl X Gustav it was to be called Academia Carolina, with the addition of the epithet *conciliatrix* to denote the university's duty of reconciling and uniting the conquered provinces with Sweden. The donation charter laid the economic foundation for the university. The academy formally received all the estates of the cathedral chapter of Lund, in all 925 freehold farms. The letter of privilege established both the privileges and the obligations of the university. It was to have the right to choose its own teachers and officials, as well as its own board of governors, the Consistory. In both criminal cases and civil disputes it would be entitled to hold trial and pass judgment; teachers and students alike were thereby exempt from the jurisdiction of the state. The constitution contained stipulations about the university's forms of government and teaching staff. The supreme governor, with the title of Chancellor, would

'A crowned lion with outstretched front paws, one holding a book, the other a sword, and between the sword and the book these words: ad utrumque.'

A description of the seal of Lund University in a document in the Stenbock manuscript collection. The motto ad utrumque, *meaning 'prepared for both', is based on a passage in* Virgil.

be appointed by the Privy Council. He would be represented in Lund by the bishop of the diocese, who was to be Vice-Chancellor ex officio.

There were to be four faculties. Each could elect its own dean for a period of six months. Initially the university rector was also elected for six months; his period of office was later lengthened. The electoral body was the Consistory, where all professors sat and had a vote. The constitution also dictated the number of teachers. There were to be four professors of theology, two of law, two of medicine, and no less than nine in the faculty of philosophy (arts and sciences). Apart from the professorships, the constitution of 1666 also mentions another type of teaching post, that of assistant lecturer (Swedish *adjunkt*).

The immediate model of the Academia Carolina was Uppsala University. This had in turn been structured after the pattern of North German universities. When it came to filling the first chairs in Lund, the professors were recruited from among the teachers of theology, philosophy, Latin, and Greek already working in the grammar school since before the Swedish conquest, as well as teachers employed by the cathedral chapter and the governor general. In these two groups all but two were Danish by birth. Five professors were summoned from German universities. Foremost among them was the Heidelberg professor Samuel Pufendorf, a man known all over Europe for his erudition. The integration of Lund into the European university sphere was marked not only by the recruitment of teachers from the continent, but also by the academic peregrinations in the opposite direction. Most Swedish academics who travelled abroad, during the rest of the seventeenth century and later, went to study in

German and Dutch universities: Greifswald, Wittenberg, Rostock, Jena, Leipzig, and Leiden. Only a few of the professors were born in Sweden, among them Anders Spole, professor of mathematics. Right from the beginning the university had an international character.

The inauguration of the Academia Carolina took place on 28th January, 1668, on the king's name-day. The medieval seat of learning had grown up in the shadow of the cathedral, where the new academy was now located. The dedication was conducted in full baroque pomp. To the sound of the cathedral bells, a military troop accompanied a profession of the professors, wearing the black silken gowns of their office. There were speeches in Latin, Swedish, and Danish. Music was provided by an orchestra of over sixty men, playing kettledrums, trumpets, and violins; a choir of fifty sang. The festivities concluded with a dinner, a gun salute, and fireworks. The ceremony attracted spectators from near and far, including foreign visitors. A detailed report of the inauguration could be read in the Hamburg newspaper *Der Nordische Merkurius*; shorter notices were printed in other German newspapers. The new media of the press carried the news of the University of Lund out over Europe.

During the inauguration ceremony, the university was presented with two silver sceptres, which are still borne in ceremonial processions today. One of them bears the words *sapientia divina* 'divine wisdom', while the other has *sapientia humana* 'human wisdom'. This proclaimed that the university should serve both the spiritual and the temporal power, both church and state.

It was a grandiose beginning, and the pledges in the donation charter concerning the economic basis for the work of the new university were magnificent. Reality, however, did not match the expectations. The financial framework was reduced right from the start, and the university was not to enjoy the revenue from all the promised chapter property. Harder times lay ahead.

If the first years of the university were nevertheless years of great promise, this was mainly because the first body of teachers included some distinguished men with a European schooling, bearers of a view of scholarship characteristic of a new age.

Old and new ideals of scholarship

The university had as its first duty to be a *seminarium ecclesiae*, an educational institution where Lutheran learning and the classical heritage would be the foundation stones. The faculty of law was organized following European models, with the two basic disciplines of Roman law and the law of nature and nations. The need for lawyers in the administration of the newly conquered province had to be satisfied, as well as the need for parish clergymen. An expression of the spirit of the new age is seen in the relatively strong representation of natural sciences and medicine; there were two chairs of mathematics, one of physics, and two of medicine.

The first decades of Lund University marked an epoch in European cultural history, with the breakthrough of new scholarly ideals of philosophical rationalism and empirical science. The founder of this new philosophy of reason was Descartes. His philosophy of nature is mechanistic: he reduces all natural phenomena to mathematical and geometrical concepts. He makes a sharp distinction between on the one hand the physical world with its dimensions, divisibility, and movement, but with no soul, and on the other hand the spiritual, immaterial world of the soul, which is without dimensions and whose chief property is thought.

On certain decisive points this new philosophy broke away from the Aristotelian doctrine which had been the accepted world view for centuries. Descartes' philosophy met strong resistance from theologians in particular. At the time when Lund University was founded, Uppsala was being torn by the Cartesian disputes between the modern schools of medicine and science and the conservative Aristotelianism of the theologians and philosophers.

The same opposition to the empirical sciences was typified by the resistance encountered by the new astronomical view of the universe. Already in the mid-sixteenth century Copernicus had taught that the sun is the centre of the universe, surrounded by Earth and the other planets, but his empirically based system was still not generally accepted; it was considered to be contrary to both the Holy Scriptures and the works of Aristotle.

The first dons at Lund University included men representing both the old and the new views of scholarship, both the guardians of Aristotelian tradition and the new men, Cartesians and Copernicans. The antagonism was scarcely conducive to peace in the young university. Among the professors who adhered to the Cartesian school were Samuel Pufendorf and Anders Spole.

Internationally, the name of Samuel Pufendorf is one the most highly reputed in the history of Lund University. He was born in Saxony in 1632, the same year as John Locke in England and Baruch Spinoza in Holland. During his student days at Leipzig and Jena he read Descartes and Thomas Hobbes. He also had an early grounding in the empirical scientific method represented by Galileo.

During his time in Jena his attention was attracted to Hugo Grotius, founder of modern natural law. According to this conception, law has its roots, not in the Roman legal system, not in Mosaic law, not in the person of the emperor, but exclusively in man's own rational nature. There is a connection via Locke and Rousseau between Pufendorf's view of human rights and that formulated in the Universal Declaration of the United Nations. As professor of natural law and international law in Heidelberg, Pufendorf came into conflict with the orthodox Lutheran theology, as well as with the emperor's antiquated view of constitutional law. The reputation of this man, who had incurred the hostility of the learned and the powerful in his own country, reached Sweden by way of Swedes studying in Europe and their tutors. He was 35 years old when — on the initiative of Magnus Gabriel de la Gardie — he accepted the invitation to become the first professor of natural law and international law in Lund.

'Londini Scanorum' is the imprint of Pufendorf's most famous work, *De Jure Naturae et Gentium* (1672). It was the first book issued by an academic press in Lund to achieve European fame. The book was written in Latin, but soon appeared in translations into the three main European languages. It has retained through the centuries an authoritative position in the study of law. Lund was also the place of publication of a more condensed textbook in which Pufendorf summarized the basic ideas in his larger work under the title *De Officio Hominis et Civis*. This too was made accessible in many languages, translated in the eighteenth century into Swedish, and used as a textbook of law throughout Europe; it remained a set book in France as late as the nineteenth century.

Pufendorf's entire philosophy was moulded by the new world view of the seventeenth century. The natural sciences and the mathematical and logical way of thinking were to show the way for law. Axioms and principles were established, and from them he derived new theoretical propositions by means of logical, geometrical proofs. Pufendorf himself was a professed Lutheran, but he never felt the need to call on the support of religion in his system of law. His work meant that the social sciences were secularized and that law declared its independence from theology.

Pufendorf's teachings were of great importance partly for their view of the relationship between church and state in his day. His opinion was that the church should be subordinate to the state in temporal matters. Such a view suited the Swedish regency well.

The publication of his major work led to the first scholarly conflict at the university. The Bishop of Lund accused the author of heresy and atheism, and Pufendorf's German-born colleague in the faculty of law, Beckman, showered him with abuse, calling him Epicurean, Pelagian, Socinian, Cartesian, Spinozian, Calvinist, polygamist, antinomist, and atheist — epithets of the sort which conservatives usually heaped upon representatives of the new philosophy. Pufendorf was not slow to answer. He defended himself against the various assailants in a number of pamphlets, later collected in a volume entitled *Eris Scandica* 'the Scandinavian strife'.

Pufendorf's secularist view of the state and the judicial system pointed the way forwards towards the Enlightenment of the eighteenth century. In an age when the main task of a university was seen to be the communication of established truths in theology and philosophy, Pufendorf, like the French group known as *les modernes*, maintained that the new scholarship was superior to the old. 'In true religion there is nothing to be changed,' he wrote, 'but in disciplines which are subject to reason, writers deserve the more praise for genius and competence the more new insights they have.'

In the faculty of philosophy the foremost name was Anders Spole. He had studied at Uppsala and then done the grand tour of Europe as tutor to three young noblemen. On this tour he came into contact with some of the outstanding scientists and mathematicians of his day. In London he met the astronomer and physicist Robert Hooke and the natural scientist Robert Boyle, both members of The Royal Society. In Bologna he met the Italian astronomer Giovanni Battista Ricciolo, known for his exact observations of the stars, but still an opponent of the Copernican system. Spole's extensive library of scientific books included the first known copy in Sweden of Newton's *Principia*.

Spole came to Lund to take up his position as *Matheseos Professor Ptolemaicus*. The old Ptolemaic view of the world was nearing its fall, however. Spole's lectures and unpublished writings are supposed to reveal that he was both a Cartesian and a Copernican, but he expressed himself with greater caution in his published works. In Lund he built an astronomical observatory on the roof of his house. He equipped it with a quadrant and a large telescope which he himself had made — during his European tour he had learnt the art of grinding lenses for optical instruments. Calendrical science fell within the scope of the professor of astronomy; Spole published almanacs for the Swedish people, both during his time in Lund and later when he had moved to become professor in Uppsala, after the dissolution of the first university in Lund.

The university's first dons were a rather heterogeneous collection of scholars of diverse origin; there were some professors from Germany, some were Danes, and a few were Swedes by origin. Struggles for precedence, typical of the age, and other internal dissensions characterized academic life right from the dedication of the university. Consistory meetings were stormy affairs. On one occasion when several of the members rose to leave the room in anger, Pufendorf's celebrated remark was: 'If there is to be such ado, then may a *Teufel* enter the Consistory.'

Apart from the professors and assistant lecturers, the university appointed a horse breaker, a fencing master, and a dance teacher; these were primarily for the service of the young nobles. There was also a salaried musician with the duty of conducting an orchestra and choir on festive academic occasions. In addition there was a language master employed to teach foreign languages. All teaching, oratory, and public defence of doctoral theses took place in Latin, as throughout Europe in this century. Dissertations and the programmes for academic and religious ceremonies were likewise written in Latin, the language of international learning.

Students and studies

According to the statutes, the professors were to hold lectures four days a week during the two terms of the academic year. The lectures consisted of dictations in Latin; students rarely had textbooks. It was stipulated that the lectures should be held 'in clear and plain language, without scholasticism, unnecessary prolixity, useless speculations, polemic, or sophistry.' Each term a lecture catalogue was printed (in Latin); the oldest extant *Elenchus Lectionum* is from 1671. Apart from the public lectures, professors held private tutorials in their homes, usually subject to a fee.

In order to matriculate at the university, applicants had to submit a testimonial from the school which they had attended; they also had to sit an entrance examination. Exceptions were made for young men from the nobility, who were accepted, often at a very early age, on account of their birth, and who received private tuition.

Before a student could proceed to legal, medical, or philosophical studies, he had to be examined in the tenets of Christianity by the theological faculty, a regulation which was a part of the university's earliest constitution, and which did not formally disappear until 1832.

Most civil professions did not require any qualifying degree. This meant that many students left the university with nothing but a testimonial to their attendance and good behaviour. The faculty of philosophy had a bachelor's degree, awarded after examination in the classical languages, history, and philosophy. An important form of teaching and examination was the *disputation*, an oral defence of a question or thesis, partly for exercise (*pro exercitio*), partly to obtain a degree (*pro gradu*). All those who wished to obtain a degree in theology, medicine, or law had to be examined in classical languages, history, and philosophy. The idea of a basic education comprising theology, the liberal arts, and science existed from the very beginning of the university. It did not disappear completely until the nineteenth century, in an ever more segmented world of knowledge.

Matriculation was preceded by a fairly brutal initiation ceremony deriving its origin from medieval universities. The freshman in his first term was called, then as now, *novitie* (or *novisch*); the usage came from North German universities, where it was an application of the monastic concept of the novice, a monk received into a religious house on probation. The university novice was dressed up as a fool and his face was blackened. A pair of horns and donkey's ears were set on his head, and two tusks in his mouth. The novices were assembled like a herd of cattle and driven through the streets until the moment when their animal emblems were removed and they were declared students. This passage rite thus conceived matriculation as a transition from an animal to a human state. The ceremony was abolished by royal decree in 1691, when all forms of overt or covert bullying were forbidden.

In the first year of the university eighty students were enrolled, and a similar number came the following year. Many of these — no less than thirty-three — were Germans; many of the professors were of German extraction too. Some students came from Denmark to train for the priesthood in Lund; the forms for examination were identical at this time in the universities of Lund and Copenhagen. But the majority of the students came and continue to come from the south of Sweden.

Students from the different provinces banded together in 'nations' with professors as supervisors. The nations had both social and educational functions. Students practised Latin oratory and the art of disputation; beer-drinking parties were also held. The nations were financed by specially established funds.

Students lodged with clergymen or their widows, with town councillors and burghers, or — in most cases — with the professors. Their life was strictly regulated by the constitution: bible reading and church attendance were compulsory. Going out at night was forbidden; after nine o'clock the students had to stay indoors and were forbidden to visit the beer cellars and taverns. Those who 'rampaged or yelled in the street' were under threat of punishment and could be thrown into the student prison (*proba*), a cellar vault behind the cathedral. The Consistory minutes record many examples of how lively the town could be at night. After a fight one Midsummer Eve in 1670, the dancing master, who was in the company of a group of students, ran his rapier through the night watchman, shouting: 'Du Hund, du muss sterben.' It was a student privilege in Sweden and elsewhere to bear a rapier.

A primitive system of scholarships developed. A 'community' was established to cater for the students, who were provided with meals according to a set menu; at table they were expected to speak Latin. As in English colleges to this day, grace was read in Latin; in addition, a hymn was sung, asking God to grant that the king and all those in authority rule well.

In his autobiography Jesper Swedberg, Bishop of Skara, gives an intimate picture of his days as a student in Lund in the 1660s. He speaks fondly of the professor with whom he lodged, who gave him evening lessons in Latin in a study which smelled of tobacco. Swedberg also speaks favourably of another of his teachers:

> While I was in Lund I had for two years in succession the great benefit of the widely famed Samuel Pufendorf. And I learned from *Jure Naturae et Gentium* and from *Officio Hominis et Civis* and from numerous authors ... how a youth should not only study books but also learn how to become an urbane, well-behaved, and useful man in human society. But to brood too much over scholastic puzzles and to do nothing but fuss about learning how to conduct polemics and fill the brain with a mass of dry questions, definitions, distinctions, and limitations is something which I have never much liked.

Swedberg then lists a number of textbooks in logic and metaphysics which he had read at university and knew like the back of his hand. 'But,' he adds, 'I do not believe that they have been any more use to me than a packet of needles.'

The dissolution and reorganization of the university

In its first form, Lund University lasted just over seven years. In June 1676 a Danish army landed in Scania. The province was to be the scene of severe ravages and campaigns in which fortunes constantly changed. The work of the university ceased and its teachers were dispersed. Several of the Danish-born professors returned forever to their homeland. Samuel Pufendorf entered the service of Karl XI (Charles XI) as historiographer royal in Stockholm, where he wrote three large works on Swedish history. Anders Spole and a few of his colleagues became professors in Uppsala.

Peace was concluded in Lund in 1679. At that time there were just three of the original teaching staff still in the town. During and after the pitched battle which had been waged against Lund, many buildings had been razed.

The economic foundation promised to the university in its charter disappeared as a result of the confiscatory policy known as Karl XI's reduction. The university had not had time to take possession of most of the property in question; now the amount was further reduced. Until the 1980s, however, nineteen of the original farms donated in the charter of 1666 were still in the possession of the university; their present tax assessment value is 30,000,000 kronor.

During the war it had become apparent that many of the townspeople and many of the peasantry still felt more Danish than Swedish, and had welcomed the Danish troops as liberators. When Sweden finally emerged victorious, Karl XI began the methodical work of incorporating the former Danish provinces into the Swedish state. The previous peace treaty drawn up in Roskilde had allowed Scania to retain its old laws and its Danish form of divine service. After the Peace of Lund, Swedish forms were now introduced in all the towns. Bishop Peder Winstrup's successor, Canutus Hahn, was one of the king's most diligent servants in the work of Swedification. It was also he who pleaded before the king that a re-established university would be an excellent tool for this purpose. On 17th June, 1682, the university was rededicated, although in more modest forms than fourteen years previously. In the autumn of the same year it resumed its work, but with reduced finances. The paltry remains of the chapter property and certain tithes were assigned for salaries and other expenses.

Instead of the seventeen professors which the constitution had provided for, the re-established university had to be content with eight, a number which gradually rose to eleven. Of the first eight professors appointed, four remained from the time of the old academy. One of these was from Greifswald, the others from Sweden proper. All new teachers were recruited within Sweden. This marked the purpose of the new university: to help in the task of Swedification. The academy of 1668 with its European profile had become a modest provincial university.

After Vice-Chancellor Canutus Hahn's entreaties with the king, there was a certain improvement in the material standards. For an initial period, right from the first dedication of the university, the cathedral chancel and chapel had served as lecture hall for most of those studying theology, law, and medicine. Exercises for philosophy students were held in the former chapter library, the Liberium to the south of the cathedral. It was in the cathedral that the Consistory met; within its walls was also housed the first book collection of the university. In a donation charter issued by Karl XI in 1688 the university received as its own building the Lundagård house. This was later appointed with a Consistory room, auditoria and a library. It was not inaugurated until 1697. Behind it lay a garden with ponds, fruit trees, and currant bushes. Plans to establish a

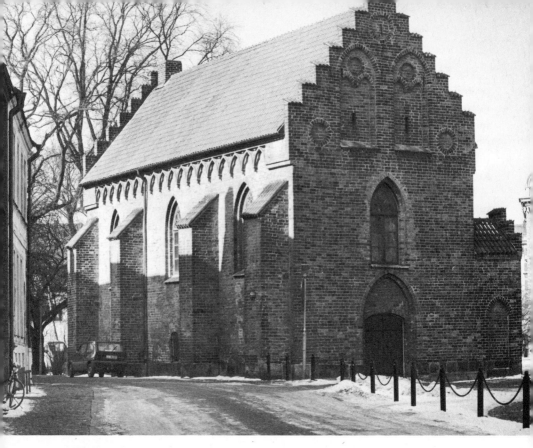

The Liberium, the medieval building by the cathedral which previously housed the cathedral chapter library.

botanical garden (*hortus botanicus*) there had to be shelved for the time being owing to lack of funds.

When the university was founded it had no library, but three years later it acquired the library of the cathedral chapter. This collection, housed since the fifteenth century in the Liberium, comprised between three and four hundred books and thirteen manuscripts. The latter included the parchment manuscripts *Liber Daticus* and *Necrologium Lundense*, both important sources for the history of the cathedral. The chapter library, reconstituted in the twentieth century, now makes up a special Bibliotheca Antiqua within the University Library.

An important addition to the university's book collection came when Karl XI donated the Gripenhielm collection in 1684. Edmund Gripenhielm, who had been the king's tutor, had amassed close to six thousand volumes during his journeys in Europe and as inspector of the Royal Library. The collection included magnificent treasures, booty from the days of the Thirty Years' War plundered from libraries in Poland, Austria, Germany, and Denmark.

War, plague, and royal visits

As in the preceding decades, the history of the university during the early eighteenth century is closely interwoven with the vicissitudes of the province. In 1709 Scania and Lund were once again invaded by Danish forces. The members of the Consistory were dispersed. The Danes established their headquarters in one professor's house, one hundred cavalrymen were quartered in the bishop's house, and the university building was transformed for a time into a store for the grain collected by the Danish troops.

Even after the Danish forces had been defeated and repulsed from the province, the hard times continued. In 1711 a fire ravaged the town, burning some forty houses. This conflagration was soon followed by the plague. Most of the work of the university was paralysed. The Consistory ordered the professors to move with their students to places in the countryside in order that 'studia academica should not totally cease.' At least one of the professors, the philosopher Andreas Rydelius, obeyed the exhortation to wander with his faithful students from village to village. Not until around 1713 could university life in Lund resume its usual course.

But a new disaster was around the corner. In 1716 King Karl XII (Charles XII) — after unsuccessful military ventures and captivity in Turkey — arrived in Lund and set up his headquarters there. For a few years Lund was the centre for the bold diplomatic activity which the king now organized and which spanned over the whole of Europe. Karl XII himself resided in one of the better professor's houses, which still stands today, now known as Karl XII's House. The royal household, officials, diplomats, and soldiers were quartered in Lund. The dons' houses were commandeered; the dons had to content themselves with a little chamber where they — as one complained — hardly had room to write a letter or to prepare their lessons. The shortage of accommodation was a problem for the students too. It was, however, the king's wish that academic life should proceed as usual. He personally visited the installation of four professors. When time permitted, he honoured lectures, orations, and disputations with his presence, showing, according to an eighteenth-century historian, 'an excellent taste for all sorts of learning and wisdom' — a surprising verdict on the warrior king.

The king's need for men led him to plan drafting into his Life Guards such 'good-for-nothing students' as wasted their time in indolence under the semblance of pursuing studies. An announcement posted on the Consistory notice board summoned all students present to be publicly examined. The move led to one of the first student riots in Lund. The students had the announcement removed, replacing it with a Latin notice which called on all students to assemble to deliberate 'about the preservation of their freedom.' No students presented themselves for the examination; they marched in a body with drawn swords to the town square. This protest led to hearings, following which some of the instigators were rusticated, others fined; two volunteered to enlist in order to escape punishment.

Karl XII left the town with his troops in June 1718. Shortly afterwards came the shot which killed the king at Fredrikshald. The peace of 1720 was celebrated in the town and at the university. Two years later Lund and its academy were visited by the new monarch Fredrik I and his consort Ulrika Eleonora on their royal tour of the country.

Chapter 2
The Eighteenth Century
The Age of Freedom and the Enlightenment

Lilla Torg, 'the little square', and the cathedral. Copperplate engraving from 1782 by J. F. Martin, based on a painting by Elias Martin. To the left in the foreground is the hostelry Härberget, to the right the home of the professor of botany Erik Gustaf Lidbeck. On the eastern side of the square is the wall around Lundagård; opposite the cathedral is the medieval cathedral school which was given to the university in 1763; it was used to house a chemistry laboratory, a musical rehearsal room, and a book auction room.

An era of peace had arrived, and with it the epoch known in Swedish history as the Age of Freedom. This was the period of early parliamentarism in Sweden. After the end of absolute monarchy with the death of Karl XII, power was transferred and concentrated in the parliament, the *Riksdag*. The end of the Age of Freedom is marked by Gustav III's revolution in 1772, when the king once again attained greater power than the Estates.

The Age of Freedom involved a revolution in both the political and the ideological climate compared with the Caroline Age. Changes in the fields of commerce, learning, and literature were felt in the university. One important development was the constitutional guarantee of the freedom of the press decreed in 1766.

The apparatus of power created by the absolute monarchs was now taken over during the Age of Freedom by a bureaucratic assembly of the Estates. The university chancellor was, now as before, a privy councillor elected by the Consistory; the election had to be approved by the sovereign. This arrangement allowed the chancellor almost dictatorial powers as an instrument of state authority.

The new chancellor of Lund University in 1728 was Count Carl Gyllenborg, who was soon to become leader of the Hat Party, one of the two political parties (the other being the Caps) which contended for power during the Age of Freedom. Carl Gyllenborg was a highly educated man who loved to play the role of *grand seigneur*; he spoke with great eloquence and conducted himself with splendid manners. He ruled the university with a patriarchal hand. On his initiative, new professorial chairs were established in each of the four faculties. Using funds raised by lotteries, he saw to it that the old university buildings were refurbished, the library expanded, and a new Consistory Hall opened. To lend lustre to the academy, he had the lecture halls adorned with portraits of kings and chancellors.

The 1730s and 1740s saw a lively discussion of the university's role in society. Utility became the goal of education. Instead of feeding youth with antiquated knowledge — by which was meant primarily the ancient languages, Greek and Hebrew — the university was supposed to give young men a thorough grounding in economics and similar practical subjects, which would be of benefit to themselves and to the country. Subjects of practical utility included natural sciences such as mineralogy, botany, zoology. It was in keeping with this mentality, which accorded a central role to the industrial development of the country, that the first chair of economics was established in Lund in the middle of the century.

In a statement formulated by a commission on education in 1750, it was declared that the chief duty of the university was to produce loyal officials to serve the state, and that learning and teaching were to be geared to the benefit of society. In phraseology which is characteristic of the mentality of the Age of Freedom, the commission conceded: 'This does not necessarily exclude the various useful secondary goals which are commonly mentioned, such as the growth of science.' It was deemed important to increase the pace of study and to restrict the intake to the universities to a level which was useful and necessary for society. It was thus proposed that candidates for admission to university be selected according to their talents.

With a view to providing a civically desirable foundation education, the commission proposed an alteration of the faculty structure. At the same time, a modernized examination system was to be introduced, with a number of new Master's degrees, qualifying graduates for such fields as appellate law, mining and metallurgy, and service in government offices; previously, students had often left university without a degree, with only a *testimonium* certifying that they had attended the university.

The proposals of the commission met with criticism in both Uppsala and Lund. In Lund it was Sven Lagerbring, the professor of history, who was responsible for most of the reports by university committees. He could not agree to the idea of restricting the purpose of academic studies to the provision of officials for the state. In words which are worth quoting he writes: 'The university is being confined within far too narrow boundaries, with only the needs of the state being considered; state officials make up a tiny minority of our people. The university is the property of all and should be for the benefit of all.'

Only a few of the commission's proposals were implemented, mainly those concerning examinations. One innovation which was to stand the test of time was the use of a regular preliminary examination (Swedish *tentamen*) to test students' knowledge before their formal final examination (*examen*) by the faculty. It was above all the chancellor who demanded a more exacting check on the university's teaching and the results it gave.

In general, the control exercised by the chancellor had an increasingly important role during the Age of Freedom. The culmination of this dominance came for Lund during a period of nine years when Nils Palmstierna, the Hat politician, was chancellor. He brought about the introduction of a fixed syllabus in both theology and law. He quite shamelessly promoted the publication and dissemination of works supporting the Hat Party in Lund University. He had the student nations subscribe to a newspaper with Hat Party sympathies, and made it the duty of a professor of law to read aloud from it during his lectures.

Like the other politicians of the age, Palmstierna spoke fondly of 'freedom'. Yet academic freedom was confined. The university teachers maintained a passive resistance, now as later, to state control, regulations, and bureaucracy.

As we have seen, the Age of Freedom was characterized by a new political climate; moreover, the spiritual climate was new. Lund University had been founded with the purpose of legitimizing the absolutism of the monarchy and guaranteeing the authority and orthodoxy of the civil service. New ideas from Europe had been tolerated only in so far as they could be incorporated into the official ideology of the state. In the Age of Freedom, however, the state and its official ideology changed in nature. This made it possible to assimilate other features carried to Sweden by new cultural currents. In the philosophy of the time, the dominant line of thought was the rationalist tradition of German thinkers like Leibniz and Wolff. With its claim of being able to reach irrefutable conclusions, Wolff's philosophy was significant for three university subjects in particular. One of these was theology, where 'natural theology' took the place of revelation theology as a defence against the attack of free-thinking; the other two subjects were law and mathematics.

Another main current in the thought of the day was empiricism. This had its origin in English science and psychology. Newton's observations had led to the erection of a system of fixed natural laws which precluded the intervention of the supernatural. Locke, the real founder of English Enlightenment philosophy, went further along the line of thought which derived knowledge from experience alone. His empiricism was to be important in fields such as education and political science, in the natural sciences and medicine.

Andreas Rydelius

Lund University in the early eighteenth century was dominated by the figure of Andreas Rydelius. He is praised in a contemporary poem as a Swedish Socrates. This is an exaggeration in the panegyric style of the day, but it is justifiable to say that he initiated in Lund a continuous Socratic tradition in philosophy which has lasted into the twentieth century. In 1710 he was appointed professor of logic and metaphysics by King Karl XII during his time in Bender, Turkey. Rydelius embarked upon a teaching career of exceptional success; students flocked to hear his lectures, often in such numbers that the lecture halls were overcrowded. He presided at a large number of disputations and wrote extensively.

Rydelius was thoroughly familiar with the main philosophical trends of his time. He adopted a mediatory position between the older rationalism and Locke's empiricism. Reason was his guiding star, as is evident from the title of his most famous work, *Nödiga förnufftz-Öfningar* ('Necessary Exercises in Reason'). An original aspect of his philosophy was his teaching about a *sensus intimus*, the 'inner feeling' of the soul, a sort of intuitive vision by which he seeks to explain the self-evident ideas which Descartes believed were innate. This was the first but not the last time an intuitive philosophy was to be taught in Lund.

His inaugural lecture bore the title *De laconismo philosophico* 'On Philosophical Laconism'. In it he opposed the scholastic heritage of the universities, the pedantic obsession with definitions which still flourished in Lund, as is evident from the examination records. Rydelius demanded that the truth be presented in clear and concise forms. He was the first among the university's professors to abandon Latin for Swedish as the language of his lectures. In Germany the philosopher Christian Thomasius had already switched from Latin to the vernacular; Fontenelle in France and Ludvig Holberg in Denmark pioneered the same trend. By talking and writing about philosophical matters in Swedish, Rydelius was the founder of Swedish philosophical prose.

Although his thinking in many ways anticipated the rationalism of the Enlightenment, he never questioned Lutheran doctrine. For many decades the intellectual atmosphere in Lund bore the mark of his eclectic philosophy.

The theological faculty

In the first half of the eighteenth century the faculty of theology had three chairs, increased to four in the middle of the century. It was the greatest of the four faculties in terms of numbers and prestige, and it paid the best salaries. The majority of those who enrolled at the university intended to enter the clergy.

Of the four professors, the first in rank, who was also dean of the cathedral, taught New Testament exegesis and moral theology, the second taught the Old Testament, confessional literature, and ecclesiastical history, the third had dogmatics as his subject, and the fourth controversy theology and homiletics.

Professors were as a rule recruited from within the university, mostly from the philosophical faculty's chairs of Greek and Oriental Languages; this path of promotion shows the importance in education of the Biblical languages. Other professors of theology (including Andreas Rydelius) came from theoretical philosophy; logic and metaphysics were still handmaidens of theology, *ancillae theologiae*. From a modern perspective, it appears more remarkable that professors could progress from mathematics and natural history to the top positions in theology, but we must bear in mind that these were all combined with the income of a prebendaryship.

Most of the teachers in the faculty had studied at Protestant universities in Germany. Important textbooks which were read and discussed at the lectures also came from German presses in Rostock, Leipzig, and Wittenberg — the latter being the source of Hafenreffer's *Loci Theologici*. Two of the Lund faculty's professors contributed textbooks of their own.

Orthodoxy was unshakeable. Theological truths were to be proved with the aid of reason. It was the age of rationalism; during the eighteenth century there was a slow transition from the eclectic Cartesianism of Rydelius to the philosophy of Wolff. But theological orthodoxy was being challenged on two fronts, by the Enlightenment and by sectarian piety.

When the fourth chair of theology was established in Lund in 1750, the subject was controversy theology and the purpose prescribed for it was the defence of the evangelical Lutheran faith against false doctrines; this meant chiefly the beliefs preached by the Pietists and Herrnhuters, new sects which had been winning followers in the south of Sweden.

The 1686 Church Act stipulated that candidates for the clergy be examined by the cathedral chapter in each diocese. The chapter in Lund included all the professors of theology and was chaired by the bishop. No one was allowed to take this examination before he could show a certificate from a professor of theology and had given proof of his knowledge of logic, metaphysics, moral philosophy, and languages; in addition, familiarity with natural sciences and economics was required later in the eighteenth century. There were thus considerable formal demands made on those who were to enter the clergy and carry education to the towns and the countryside.

The revival of legal studies

The faculty of law, which had been organized on European models and which had relied heavily on foreign teachers during its initial phase, acquired a more Swedish character and orientation after the 1680s. Swedish law gained precedence, Roman law declined in importance, and the academic lawyers were increasingly occupied with the Swedification process in the southern provinces. After the rededication of the university in 1682, the faculty of law had only one professor. His subject included both Swedish and Roman law. The few students of law were also taught by the professor of practical philosophy.

During the war years at the start of the eighteenth century the students had complained that *juris studium* had been discontinued. It was revived by David Nehrman, called Ehrenstråhle after he was raised to the peerage. He was the real founder of Swedish legal science. He had begun his studies in Lund and continued at Dutch and German universities. At Halle he had heard the famous Christian Thomasius, philosopher of the Enlightenment and teacher of natural law.

When appointed professor in 1720, he revived and renewed the traditional ideas of natural law from Pufendorf's days; the latter's monographs and textbooks were still in use at the university, in Latin or in Swedish translations. Natural law, the doctrine of the original social contract between the people and their rulers, had been used during the Caroline era to legitimize monarchy. The same doctrine was now used as an argument against absolute monarchy. John Locke had been one of those who had interpreted natural law to mean that power in society actually belonged to the people. It was in an ideological climate influenced by such thoughts that the Swedish constitution and form of government in the Age of Freedom came about. Nehrman too interpreted natural law in this spirit.

He accorded little space in his teaching to Roman law and legal tradition; in his opinion, the Roman *Corpus Juris* was 'a disorderly collection'; moreover, Roman and Swedish law had as little in common as Catholic and Protestant belief. Nehrman therefore devoted his lectures to Swedish law and legal tradition, on which he then based his *Inledning till den svenska jurisprudentiam civilem* ('Introduction to Swedish Civil Jurisprudence'), which remained a textbook until the 1840s. He used his mother tongue in all his lectures and writings. What Rydelius did for Swedish philosophical prose, Nehrman did for the language of law.

Nehrman-Ehrenstråhle's career can be divided into two halves. During the first, up to 1734, he saw it as his duty to interpret for his students the old laws of Sweden, using historical and philological methods to elucidate the laws which were still valid. After the legal reform of 1734, he devoted his lectures to a section-by-section interpretation of the new laws, which he had helped to formulate.

An important reform in legal studies came in Nehrman's time and partly on his initiative: the introduction of a proper law examination.

The early study of medicine in Lund

According to the original constitution of the university, the faculty of medicine was to have two professors. One was to be a *practicus*, in charge of surgery and pharmacology. The other was to be responsible for teaching anatomy and holding dissections; most of the natural sciences also fell within his sphere: physics, chemistry, and botany — knowledge of herbs and medicine have gone hand in hand since the dawn of culture. Both professors were to lecture alternately on passages from Hippocrates and Galen.

The universities of Leiden and Copenhagen in particular, as well as the German universities, were the strongholds of medical science at the close of the seventeenth century. Two professors of theoretical medicine during the earliest days of Lund University had taken their doctorates in Leiden. In Copenhagen the famous names were Niels Stensen and Thomas Bartholin. Bartholin developed in his writings and lectures the idea that diseases were associated with anatomical changes which could be confirmed by autopsy. He made findings of fundamental importance in anatomy and pathology; he is famous for his discovery of the lymphatic gland.

One pupil of Bartholin's was Erasmus Sack, who adopted the name Sackensköld on being raised to the peerage. After the restoration of the university in 1682, when the faculty of medicine had been reduced to a single professorship, Sackensköld alone was responsible for the training of all doctors.

The first noteworthy professor of medicine in the early eighteenth century was Johan Jacob Döbelius. After receiving his doctorate in his native town, Rostock, he continued his studies at German universities and in Copenhagen. As a provincial doctor in Scania he discovered the mineral spring at Ramlösa; he subsequently ran this spa. In this way his face has become familiar to posterity; it can still be seen on the label of every bottle of Ramlösa mineral water. It was under his supervision that the previously planned botanical gardens with medicinal plants were founded north of the university building. On his initiative too came an anatomical theatre on the second floor of the university building in Lundagård.

Döbelius's successor as professor of practical medicine was Eberhard Rosén-Rosenblad. In order to learn the latest in medical science of his day, he had made an extensive tour of Europe, which had brought him to Göttingen, the foremost German university of the day, founded in 1728. All the faculties there boasted major scholars. The professor of medicine, anatomy, and surgery was the Swiss Albrecht von Haller. He was also in charge of the anatomical theatre and the botanical gardens. Moreover, he had founded the university's first learned society, Die Gesellschaft der Wissenschaften, and he was editor of its transactions. Rosén-Rosenblad established close contact with this outstanding anatomist and physiologist. The two men became friends and continued to correspond.

Beside Haller, it was Herman Boerhaave who dominated medical thought during the eighteenth century. Boerhaave, the learned doctor from Leiden, who also taught medicine to Linnaeus, had developed a theory of pathology based on the body's 'fibres' and fluids, among these the consistency of the blood. Boerhaave's ideas were used by Eberhard Rosén-Rosenblad in his syllabus. In his lectures, which were famed for their clarity and cogency, he dealt with practically all the fields of contemporary medicine: pathology, anatomy, physiology, and pharmacology.

It was thanks to Rosenblad that the town acquired its first hospital, intended also as a university clinic. This *nosocomium academicum*, the modest forerunner of today's huge hospital, could care for at most ten patients.

The faculty of philosophy

According to the university constitution the philosophy faculty was to have six ordinary professorships. Further teaching posts came in the course of the eighteenth century, indicating the growing interest in science and economics.

In 1728 a chair was created for Kilian Stobaeus the Elder, to teach natural philosophy and experimental physics. Stobaeus came from one of the oldest families associated with the university; no less than five professors at Lund have borne that name. He began his studies in medicine with Döbelius, became doctor of medicine in Lund, and was acting professor of medicine for a time. In the syllabus which he outlined he favoured an empirical approach to the subject; he considered that lecturing on Hippocrates and Galen, as the constitution prescribed, was as irrelevant as studying the Koran in theology.

His research on nature consisted of extensive collecting activity. His famous Museum Stobaeanum, a natural history collection which he founded in 1735, was donated by him to the university. Collections like this provided the material needed by later generations of botanists, zoologists, and geologists in their more systematic research.

Stobaeus's most famous pupil was Carl von Linné, known to the world as Linnaeus; he has left us the following picture of the Stobaean collection in his autobiography: 'A fine Museum of all sorts of Naturalia: Stones, Shells, Birds,

One of the most widely distributed portraits of a private Swedish citizen, the professor of medicine Johan Jacob Döbelius (1647–1743), founder of Ramlösa Spa, which was opened to the public in 1707.

and Herbaria.' The collection was to become the foundation of the university's later museums of natural history, archeology, and history. The remains of the Stobaean collection which have survived to our day include exotic shells, fish, stuffed birds, neuroptera, butterflies, a few fossils, and rock samples.

During his brief period of study in Lund, Linnaeus lived with Stobaeus in his house by the cathedral. From his landlord he learned such arts as pressing flowers for his herbarium. He pursued his early studies in Stobaeus's well-appointed library, which comprised 1,700 volumes. Linnaeus himself tells a famous story of how he borrowed books from this library without permission and was discovered one night with the wax candle burning in his bedroom. The outcome was that the young scholar was permitted to quench his thirst for knowledge with unrestricted access to the library during the daylight hours, on top of which he was allowed to dine with Stobaeus free of charge. Linnaeus writes in his autobiographical notes of his teacher: 'I shall be obliged to this gentleman as long as I live for the love he had for me, for he loved me more as a son than as a disciple.' After he had left Lund, Linnaeus corresponded with Stobaeus; letters have survived to show that Stobaeus was also in touch with distinguished foreign scholars, chiefly in Denmark, but also with more distant authorities, such as the superintendent of the botanical gardens in Bologna.

It was during Linnaeus's years of study in Lund that Stobaeus was appointed to the extraordinary chair of natural philosophy and experimental physics. Notes from his lectures show that his view of physics was still Cartesian, not Newtonian. After a few years he moved to an ordinary professorship in history, a change which was forced upon him primarily for financial reasons. He lectured on Swedish customs and antiquities, and presented in a dissertation some of the most remarkable documents in the University Library, among them *Liber Daticus* and *Necrologium Lundense*. In his archaeological studies he applied elementary comparative methods; he was one of the first to point out that flint tools must have been used before iron tools in Scandinavia. In all the fields of learning which he touched he represented the empiricism of the times.

England, with its Royal Society, was the centre of scientific and medical research of the day. Among the doctors and natural historians who visited England was Gustaf Harmens, from the 1730s professor of medicine and experimental philosophy in Lund. As tutor to a young noble he had been in Oxford and Cambridge, where he made the acquaintance of several important doctors. On a later trip he met Sir Hans Sloane, President of the Royal Society, an eminent physician who was also known for his natural history collections which were to become the basis of the future British Museum. Another scholar who had gone to England for his education in modern science was the physicist and engineer Mårten Triewald; it is probable that he met Newton in person. While in England Triewald bought a collection of physics instruments which he demonstrated during public lectures in Stockholm to a large and interested audience. His assistant at the lectures was a young mechanic called Daniel Menlös.

Both Triewald's collection of instruments and Daniel Menlös later ended up in Lund in a remarkable way. Daniel Menlös offered to buy the instruments and donate them to the university in return for a professorship in mathematics — a form of academic promotion which was evidently considered permissible in the Age of Freedom. Professor Menlös lectured on mathematics, geometry, mathematical geography, and physics. Notes surviving from his physics lectures show that he followed Newton on every point: the laws of gravity, motion, and the refraction of light.

Of the original 327 instruments in the Triewald collection some 70 survive to this day (preserved in the Technical Museum in Malmö). The most remarkable is one of the pumps which von Guericke used in Regensburg to pump the air out of the celebrated 'Magdeburg Hemisphere', which sixteen pairs of horses could not manage to draw apart. The collection also included one of the oldest microscopes and a machine for creating static electricity.

The Triewald collection contained only three astronomical instruments. The history of astronomical observation in Lund does not begin properly until 1749, when Nils Schenmark was appointed *astronomiae observator*, and was made professor in 1763. A room over the stairwell in the round tower of the university building was equipped as an observatory. A tube measuring eighteen French feet in length was set up beside a sixteen-inch reflecting telescope and a pendulum clock for timing the observations. In 1751 the Academy of Sciences

One of the two surviving examples of Otto von Guericke's pump, the most famous piece of apparatus in the Triewald collection which Daniel Menlös brought to Lund.

was commissioned, along with French astronomers, to measure the distance of the moon from the earth, as well as to observe Mars and Venus to determine their parallaxes. When the planet Venus passed the solar disc during the passage of Venus ten years later, organized observations from several places made it possible to determine the parallax of the sun; Schenmark took part in this work too. The results were published in Paris. Beside his astronomical observations Schenmark continued the meteorological observations which his predecessor had begun; one reason for these was the practical value they had for the navy.

A task of a purely mathematical nature which occupied Schenmark was the compilation of series of primary numbers; he calculated in all 1,000,800. The result was sent not only to the Swedish Academy of Sciences but also to corresponding bodies in Paris and St Petersburg. Schenmark's lectures were of an encyclopaedic nature, covering mathematics, physics, and hydraulics, as well as astronomy. They are preserved in seventeen handwritten volumes.

Sven Lagerbring and Swedish history

Sven Bring, later raised to the peerage as Lagerbring, became professor of history in 1742, succeeding Kilian Stobaeus the Elder. During his early years as professor, Lagerbring presided at almost two hundred doctoral disputations. Many were topographical dissertations, particularly concerning Scanian local history, while others were editions of documentary sources. Lagerbring was the first to edit those two works of such importance for the history of the diocese of Lund, *Necrologium Lundense* and *Liber Daticus Lundensis*.

Lagerbring's *magnum opus* is his *Svea Rikes Historia* ('History of the Kingdom of Sweden'), written with an Enlightenment perspective on the course of history. In his description of Sweden's earliest history he relies faithfully on the accounts of Snorri Sturluson, the *Ynglinga saga*, and the Icelandic sagas. In the second part, however, when he reaches the Christian Middle Ages and a better documented period of history, he begins to examine the sources critically. He dismisses fanciful suppositions which had attained the status of historical facts. 'In particular,' he writes, 'one must beware of taking the guesses of previous writers for undoubted truths. An unfounded opinion or an incorrect detail must not be metamorphosed through time into an undisputed historical fact.' He thus formulates one of the fundamental theses of critical historiography.

Lagerbring, who devoted a dissertation to a subject typical of the age, the uses and utility of history, did not shrink from moral reflections on the past in his historical writings. One of his models was the Danish historian Ludvig Holberg, a man of the Enlightenment who was active both as a playwright and a professor of history in Copenhagen. Like Holberg, he had been influenced by French Enlightenment writers like Pierre Bayle and Voltaire. Nevertheless, like older historians of Bossuet's type, he remained firm in the conviction that Providence ultimately links the fate of the nations and the world.

Lagerbring was one of the first literary Scandinavians. It is not only his position as a disciple of Holberg which justifies this judgment. He corresponded with historians in Denmark and also studied in Copenhagen. He was moreover the first scholar from Lund to be elected to Queen Lovisa Ulrika's Academy of Literature, History, and Antiquity. His reputation at his own university was distinguished. At his death, Anders Jahan Retzius held a commemorative speech which began rhetorically: 'Who can deny that Lund has lost its crown?'

Scenes of the eighteenth-century university town

Linnaeus visited Lund on his Scanian tour in June 1749. He found the town an academic pastoral tableau in the summertime, where one could hear the cowherds in the mornings blowing their horns as the cattle were driven out to graze. He compared his memories of a previous stay there as a student: 'The academy in Lund had been improved so considerably during the one-and-twenty years since I had studied there that I could scarcely recognize it.' His attention was primarily attracted by the park which had been newly planted two years previously. 'Lundagård, which was laid out in front of the university by our unparalleled Surveyor to the Royal Household, Baron Hårleman, was matchlessly splendid with the many sorts of tree with which it was adorned, besides which it was surrounded by a solid wall and closed with three fine iron gates.' After designs by the eminent Rococo chateau builder and landscape gardener, Carl Hårleman, the avenues had been laid out in fan-shaped geometrical patterns which by and large survive today.

Before the park was laid out, the eight-foot-high wall had been built around Lundagård, totally enclosing it. The wall had a symbolic function, dividing 'town' from 'gown'. A short stretch of the wall, or more accurately a projection

The sole survivor of the three gates in the wall around Lundagård, now the main entrance into the Kulturen museum. Wrought iron work by Setterström, a Stockholm smith, commissioned by Chancellor Carl Gyllenborg.

of it around the original botanical gardens, is still extant on the south side of Paradisgatan. One of the three gates, the eastern one, also stands to this day. It is of wrought iron, its crest adorned with a gilded crown. It is now the main entrance to the Kulturen museum.

An orangery in the ornate French style was erected by the north wall of the old botanical gardens. Bay-berry trees, cedars, almond trees, aloes, and other rare trees were planted there in clay pots and iron urns. In charge of the botanical gardens and the orangerie in the mid-century period was Erik Gustaf Lidbeck. Some years previously he had been companion and secretary to Linnaeus on his journey though Västergötland, and as assistant lecturer in medicine at the university he taught botany, natural history, and mineralogy; later he was to become professor of natural history. In his capacity as superintendent of the botanic gardens (*praefectus horti*) he was instructed by the Academy of Sciences to propagate useful plants for the household, for medicine, and for dyeing. He was also supposed to present his results to the Estates General; the spirit of mercantilism required that the findings of natural history be directed towards practical uses. Thousands of mulberry bushes were planted on university land and on private gardens for the cultivation of silk worms. The Manufacturing Board had promised premiums to home-produced silk. Lidbeck set to work enthusiastically and wrote in the transactions of the Academy of Sciences about the mulberry plantations in Scania and the results which the industrious silkworms were expected to produce. The experiment was not very successful; some cold winters in the 1780s froze most of the trees; a few metres of silk made from thread produced in Lund is all that remains from the grandiose project with its state patronage.

Jubilee celebrations. A review of the first century

The centennial of the university was celebrated with pomp and festivity in Lund in the summer of 1768. Like the inauguration ceremony, the centennial was celebrated in the cathedral chancel, where the theology professors still held their lectures. A printed programme stated the order of the ceremonies and processions. The festivities were opened with an eight-gun salute, and trumpet and timpani music played from the balcony of the observatory.

After a day's interval for Midsummer Day the festivities continued with the conferring of degrees, a different day for each faculty. The graduation ceremony was colourful: the hats worn by the doctors of law were adorned with white silk, blue ribbons, and golden tassels. Graduates in medicine had light blue silk on their hats, with white ribbons and roses; the philosophers received their wreaths (as they still do today). The graduation ceremony included several features since dropped. One of these was the closing of the books: at one point in the ritual the newly graduated doctors slammed shut an open book which they held in their hand, as a sign that they now mastered their subject. Another ritual which has vanished was the doctoral interrogation; questions were asked and answered in Latin.

It was a modest small-town university which commemorated its centennial with such pomp. At this time the theology faculty had four professors, law had one, medicine had two. The faculty of philosophy boasted no less than nine.

There were eleven dons with the rank of assistant lecturer (*adjunkt*) and eight with the rank of senior lecturer (*docent*). The latter post had developed gradually out of the *jus docendi*, the right to teach which the university constitution granted to all those with a master's or doctor's degree. The *docent* remained an important part of the university hierarchy until 1985. Apart from these categories of teacher, there was also the language master (teaching French, Spanish, and English), the choirmaster, the riding master, the fencing master, and the dancing master.

In accordance with the salary stipulations, professors were still paid 300 barrels of grain, half rye and half barley. The professors of theology had their prebendal livings, as did a few of the philosophy professors.

During the hundred years which had passed since the foundation of the university, a total of eight thousand students had been enrolled. During the first decades of the eighteenth century, the number of new students matriculating each year fluctuated between fifty and a hundred. After the 1730s the figure rose, falling again in the middle of the century; in the jubilee year of 1768 it had risen to 127, and at the close of the century the figure was only slightly lower. The total number of students at the university in any one year was never more than five hundred.

There were seven student nations. For the whole of the eighteenth century, on average half of the students came from the southern provinces of Sweden. More than a third were clergymen's sons. Over half of the students leaving the university entered professions in church, school, or university, but in the course of the century there was a slow shift in the proportions: the number of clergymen fell while those entering civil professions increased in number.

Student life was still governed by strict rules, which were often broken. The students of the day were as young as modern high-school students, between 15 and 20. The rules dictated that they should be at home in their lodgings after nine o'clock in wintertime, ten o'clock in the summer. Yet the pitch-dark night streets, with nearly no lighting, enticed students to 'break curfew' and get into 'night rows'. This could lead to clashes between the students and their town rivals, the apprentices and journeymen, sometimes also fights between different student nations. The students were still entitled to carry swords, and they were often prepared to draw them when provoked. The guilty parties faced a hearing in the Consistory, which could lead to imprisonment in the *proba*, in serious cases even to rustication. There were other forms of student pranks and provocations. There often appeared on the university notice board, the *tabula publica*, libellous pamphlets defaming the university teachers or the town magistrate. Other forms of entertainment were rather limited; card playing was not permitted, but it did take place in public taverns or private homes. In 1759 a public prohibition was issued against performances by troupes of actors and travelling artistes in term time.

Teaching was still mostly in the form of lectures. In the seventeenth century the lectures in every faculty had been in Latin; Swedish was now beginning to compete, earlier in Lund than in Uppsala. The Consistory had suggested in a report of 1723 that Swedish should be used in both lectures and disputations. Students were still, however, examined in Latin; the overwhelming majority of dissertations were written and publicly defended in Latin. As before, the dissertations were usually written by the professor; he presided at the disputation while the doctoral candidate (*respondent*) defended the dissertation against specially appointed opponents. Only in economic subjects did occasional dissertations appear in Swedish, and the university programme was sometimes issued in both languages.

From the beginning of the century, however, French was gaining ground. A French student in Lund was appointed as language master. In the 1770s the first lecturer in French and English was appointed. The broader linguistic perspective reflects changes in the general cultural and scholarly spectrum in the course of the eighteenth century.

University learning and the culture of the capital

The academic world in Sweden was still considered a bastion of Latin supremacy. The attack on the academic cult of Latin as an antiquated form of education came from the Stockholm press. The antagonism between the French-influenced fashionable culture of the capital and the archaic scholarship of the university found expression already in the middle of the century, and it was heightened in the second half of the eighteenth century. One target of the new criticism was the disputation, which was condemned as an outmoded relic of the Latin exercises of bygone days. It was said that the young men still had to propound syllogisms after Plenning's *Logica*, know the names of all the tropes and figures in the *Rhetorica* of Vossius, and learn by heart the definitions in the *Compendium Ethicum* of Omeis. This method, it was claimed, did not teach them how to handle concepts, express their thoughts, or learn their obligations as a citizen and a human being.

Aggressive journalists forgot to mention in their vehement and often witty articles that the eighteenth-century university was a focus of the new Enlightenment. 'The sciences have brought enlightenment to the people who wander in the darkness,' Linnaeus had said, and the new light really had begun to shine in the dark lecture halls of Lund University. A professor of physics in Lund was the first person in Sweden to defend in public the Copernican view of the universe; in a disputation in 1714 he entered into polemics with the astrologers' belief in the influence of the heavenly bodies on the fortunes of men. In another disputation the old notions about alchemy were contested. Newton's physics had become generally accepted, and Aristotle's authority in ethics and law had been pronounced obsolete by a professor of natural law in the mid-eighteenth century.

Yet another thirty years were to elapse before the provincial universities of Uppsala and Lund were to take over the leadership in the intellectual and literary debate. By then the romantic revolution in thought, art, and science had led to a complete change of system, which in the history of philosophy is usually derived from Kant and his Copernican revolution.

The change in philosophical system

Immanuel Kant was introduced early to Lund. His tract on aesthetics, *Beobachtungen über das Gefühl des Schönen und Erhabenen*, was translated to Swedish and published in *Lunds Weckoblad* in 1777. In the same year Mattheus Fremling became assistant lecturer in philosophy in Lund, and later professor of theoretical philosophy. It was Fremling, together with his colleague in the chair of practical philosophy, Lars Peter Munthe, who introduced Kant to the young generation of students in a series of lectures. Fremling had taken his master's degree in 1770 at Greifswald, where he may have come across the work of Kant, whom he later described as one of the most profound logicians and metaphysicians of the day. In the 1790s Fremling lectured on Kant's *Kritik der reinen Vernunft*. He himself was somewhat critical of the ideas he was presenting, and he dismissed Kant's doctrine of space and his moral philosophy with the categorical imperative..

Fremling continued to lecture into the next century on Fichte's idealism and Schelling's philosophy of nature and identity. The latter led to an intervention by the then chancellor of the university, who feared that 'young heads might be bewildered.' Fremling successfully defended his academic freedom to teach what he chose. He saw it as his duty, as he said, 'incessantly to advance with the times, to abandon old errors without being seduced by new ones.' He thus championed a Lundensian philosophical tradition which was not tied to any school of thought.

A contemporary of Fremling's was Lars Peter Munthe, whose title was *juris et philosophiae practicae professor*. In his attacks on Wolffian rationalism, Munthe took his weapons from the English moral-sense philosophers, Hutcheson, Smith, and others. At the same time he developed an older Lund tradition derived from Andreas Rydelius and his teaching on reason and the senses. From the 1790s he vigorously defended Kant's practical philosophy, which he tried to reconcile with his previous moral-sense approach.

Yet a third Lund scholar was influenced by the English moral-sense school and the German Kantian philosophy. This was Anders Lidbeck, professor of aesthetics from 1801. His career is a fine example of the academic mobility which still characterized the age. After taking his master's degree (as *primus*) he became lecturer in natural history. He also became famous for his knowledge of *belles lettres*, which he was entrusted to teach; the king had decreed that this subject should be available at the university, linked to the post of university librarian. Lidbeck did considerable work for the library, including writing a history of its early days.

His lectures on 'Aesthetics and Related Matters' took as a point of departure the Brunswick professor Eschenburg and his *Theorie der schönen Künste*, a theory which was then in high esteem in Lund, as well as in Copenhagen and Uppsala. In 1796 he lectured on the aesthetics in Kant's *Kritik der Urtheilskraft*. Like many of his contemporaries, Lidbeck sought a compromise between old and new. He followed Schiller, who strove to use the arts in moral education in order to harmonize man's sensual and rational nature.

New philological scholarship

Germany was the source of new ideas in more than just philosophy and aesthetics; this neo-humanist age also saw new directions in the study of language. Göttingen, the trend-setting German university, was the focus of a renewed interest in antiquity, chiefly through Christian Gottlob Heyne, professor of oratory. His lectures and his editions of classical authors, among them Homer, Pindar, and Virgil, kept the revived interest in the subject on the crest of a wave which bore it into the next century.

Another of the foremost representatives of neo-classicism in Germany was

Johann August Ernesti, professor of classical literature and oratory at Leipzig; he was known as the German Cicero. There was at the same time a revival in the study of oriental languages, led by Johann David Michaelis, professor of philosophy and oriental languages at Göttingen. Both of these men had pupils who went on to become outstanding teachers at the University of Lund.

One of Ernesti's pupils was Johan Lundblad, who had received a scholarship to study in Germany in the 1770s. This was right in the middle of the Werther period, and Lundblad was profoundly influenced by the new sentimental trend. As Ernesti's pupil he took his doctorate in Leipzig and then continued his studies in Halle and Greifswald. On his return to Sweden he became lecturer and later professor in Latin oratory and poetry. He represented the early type of neo-classicism which still found its models and ideals in Latin literature. He himself wrote Latin verse and Ciceronian prose which displayed perfect mastery of the forms. Through his efforts Lund remained one of the last reserves of classical Latin oratory in Europe.

At the same time, oriental languages had a distinguished representative in Mathias Norberg. He had spent his early years as a student in Uppsala, where he became lecturer in Greek. Royal support enabled him to undertake a tour of Europe, which took him by way of Germany, Holland, England, and France to Italy. In the Paris library he discovered an oriental manuscript which he was to edit under the title *Liber Adami*, a work which made his name famous. In the Ambrosian Library in Milan he made a transcript of a little-known manuscript of the Old Testament, Codex Syriaco-Hexaplaris.

Norberg continued his linguistic studies in Turkey under various Turkish scholars. At the same time he immersed himself in the history of religion. On his way home to Sweden he delivered a lecture to a learned society in Göttingen (who later printed it in their transactions) about the religion and language of the Sabaean people of southern Arabia. In Göttingen he was in close contact with the German oracle on oriental languages, the Johann David Michaelis mentioned above.

Mathias Norberg was appointed professor of Greek and Oriental Languages in Lund in 1780. He began his editing career by publishing the codex which he had found in Milan, the Syrian text of some of the Old Testament prophets, with an accompanying translation into Latin. His eagerly awaited *magnum opus*, the translation of *Liber Adami*, now known as *Ginzā* ('Treasury'), was preceded by a large number of doctoral dissertations in Latin supervised by Norberg. The entire work was not completed until the first decade of the nineteenth century. When judged by modern philological standards, Norberg's translation has its flaws. Nevertheless, in the age of Romanticism which pervaded Sweden and the rest of Europe, with poets drawn towards the Orient and its religious monuments, Adam's Book was highly valued. Michaelis himself said that he found in it 'the true riches of the Orient.' The poet and professor Esaias Tegnér, who had studied Greek under Norberg, characterized him as the wise patriarch of the university: 'Thou friend of the Orient and credit to Scandinavia.'

Sciences in the eighteenth century. The first learned society in Lund

The flowering of the natural sciences in Uppsala in the Age of Freedom, with Linnaeus, Scheele, and Torbern Bergmann, had no counterpart in Lund. It was not until Anders Jahan Retzius that the university acquired a scholar who, like Linnaeus, had a mastery of the three kingdoms of nature — animal, vegetable, and mineral. 'My science,' he said, 'is an ocean.'

Retzius was appointed ordinary professor in 1786, first of economics, later of natural history and economics, and finally also of chemistry. Before this, in his years as a lecturer in chemistry, he had worked together with a brilliant chemist, Carl Wilhelm Scheele, partly during Scheele's time as a pharmacist in Malmö. Retzius and Scheele together managed to produce tartaric acid in a crystalline form. Another of Retzius's chemical analyses concerned citric acid, now once more the object of biochemical interest.

His lectures dealt by turns with zoology, botany, mineralogy, and chemistry. In these and in his published works he has as his main interest the description and organization of the various spheres of natural history. He had an expanded and systematically improved edition of Linnaeus's Swedish fauna published in Leipzig; the book covered mammals, birds, amphibians, and fish, under the title *Fauna Sueciae, pars prima*. His botanical publications included a study of the flora of Scania and the internationally acknowledged *Observationes Botanicae* (1779–91), six folio volumes with coloured copperplate engravings. He had trees and bushes from Siberia and North America planted in the Botanical Gardens in Lund. A typical indication of the utilitarian botany of the age — which was a subject combined with economics — was the trend in his work *Flora Oeconomica Sveciae*, a manual of self-sufficiency for agrarian Sweden.

Retzius collected and systematized fossil finds from the peat bogs of Scania. His essay on these finds laid the foundation of the quaternary palaeontology which has found a citadel in Lund. He also collected archaeological antiquities;

on his initiative the old Stobaean collection was divided into two museums, one for natural history, one for cultural history. He donated to the former his herbarium with over 20,000 species, as well as his zoological and geological collections; to the latter he donated his collection of antiquities.

Retzius was the last person in Sweden whose scholarship covered the entire scope of natural history; after his death the professorship which he had held was divided into three.

The eighteenth century was the age of learned societies. In Lund it was Retzius who took the initiative to found in 1772 the university's oldest society still in existence, the Physiographical Society. Physiography means the description of natural phenomena, and the foundation charter declared that the members of the society were to devote their attention primarily to the study and illumination of the natural history and economy of Scania; the scope was later widened to include all the branches of science and medicine.

Danish university men were soon elected as members of the society, a sign of the renewed contacts with the University of Copenhagen. Links between Lund and Copenhagen had in fact never been competely severed, despite occasional chills in political relations between Sweden and Denmark. Historians in Lund and Copenhagen established contacts at an early stage, as did scholars in medicine, natural history, and philology.

From Denmark came the first member of a family which was to play an important role in the printing history of the university, Carl Gustaf Berling. He came from the same family which in Denmark had founded the Berling printing house and *Berlingske Tidende*, a daily newspaper which is still being published. When Berling came to Lund, he applied to the university authorities in the 1740s for permission to set up a printing house in the town. Among publications which appeared in the eighteenth century were Sven Lagerbring's *Svensk historia*, a number of academic programmes and speeches, the weekly *Lunds Weckoblad* (from 1775), devotional manuals, popular writings, and coloured woodcuts. The same family continued for four generations to run the Berling printing house, which was responsible for the publication of most of the academic work of the university.

Lund University, which had originally been founded as a national counterpart to the university in the Danish capital, had begun to enter into ever closer relations with its neighbour across the sound. The revived contacts point the way forwards to the more vigorous literary, cultural, and political contacts which were to characterize the atmosphere in the student town in the following century.

Sturm und Drang. Echoes of the French Revolution

The philosophy of the Enlightenment, the critical and radical spirit which had developed on French soil with Voltaire and the *encyclopédistes*, did not begin to gain ground in Sweden before the reign of Gustav III (1771–1792). It influenced a narrow circle of intellectuals and writers, mostly in Stockholm, the press, the court, and Gustav III's Academy. But it never caught on in the universities.

By contrast, the pre-Romantic trend, the age of *Sturm und Drang* with its emotional revolt against sterile intellectualism, quickly met with an enthusiastic response from the young generation of students. In the 1770s Lund admitted to the law faculty two young men who were to become the leading figures in Swedish pre-Romanticism, Thomas Thorild and Bengt Lidner.

This was the decade of sentimental friendship and the worship of nature. Thorild became close friends with some of his contemporaries, their affection documented in surviving letters which are typical of the age. One of his nearest friends was the young Johan Lundblad, newly returned home from a Germany in the grip of Werther fever. Thorild reacted with youthful vigour against the general atmosphere of compulsion and pedantry which he found in the university; he felt morally dead in this 'desert of scholarship' with its 'squabbles' and 'terrible orthodoxies.'

Thorild and Lidner took an active part in the meetings of the student nations, where orations and disputations were still the order of the day. Thorild held a remarkable speech in 1778, in which he presented the fundaments of his future philosophy, stated his position on contemporary thinkers, chiefly Rousseau, defended freedom of thought, and condemned the Sorbonne. Much later his enthusiasm for French ideas of liberty were to lead to exile from Sweden. In 1795 he became professor of philosophy at the University of Greifswald, which was still Swedish; while there he established close contacts with one of the pioneers of Romanticism, J.G. von Herder. At a disputation Bengt Lidner defended a number of theses, among them the Latin maxim *in lacrymis voluptas* 'pleasure in tears'.

Thorild and Lidner were two stormy petrels of the new generation. There are indications of a radicalization of the student body in the 1790s, after the French Revolution. From the start of that decade the students began to wear a cockade in their hats, long before the time of the white student cap. A student revolt in 1793 was viewed by the public prosecutor as a radical political demonstration. One of the students was accused of singing a political ditty attacking the nobility, with echoes of the French revolutionary song 'Ça ira'. One spring morning the following year a tree of freedom was discovered planted in Lundagård, with a notice saying *L'arbre chéri sacrifié à la liberté*. On both occasions the university vice-chancellor tried to make light of the events, but the powers that were in the capital, Reuterholm and Duke Karl (who led the regency after the assassination of Gustav III), showed their discontent with the students by omitting to visit Lund on their tour of Scania.

The political undercurrents of revolt would find new forms of expression in the coming century. But it was in science and letters that a revolution was accomplished in the Swedish Romantic Age, the nineteenth century.

Chapter 3
The Nineteenth Century
From Romanticism to Positivism

The wall around Lundagård, from a view of Sandgatan in the 1820s. To the left is the house which was to become the first home of the Academic Union. Left of the Lundagård building is the new university annexe, built early in the nineteenth century and demolished in 1897. Of the people by the wall, the most voluminous is, according to a contemporary tradition, the professor of philosophy, Mattheus Fremling.

The driving forces behind the cultural revolution of Romanticism came primarily from German philosophers, scholars, and poets. A new organic and holistic view opposed the mechanistic explanations of previous generations of scholars, and became fundamental for the natural sciences, medicine, law, and the arts.

If the capital had been the centre of cultural life in the Gustavian era, the romantic period shifted the centre of gravity to the universities. In Germany the universities of Jena and Heidelberg had been bulwarks of the romantic movement. Uppsala and Lund played a corresponding role in Sweden. It was here that people studied philosophical idealism, Schelling, Schleiermacher, Fichte, and later Hegel. It was here that the rigid theological dogmatism was slowly freed from the grip of rationalism and neology. It was here that Greek antiquity was rediscovered, interpreted in the idealistic spirit of Winckelmann's neo-humanism. It was here that national history was studied and expounded as a reflection of the inward life of the nation. It was here that the new poems were composed and read.

During the Napeolonic Wars the Germans had founded a new university in Berlin as a symbol of national unity. Its programme was elaborated by men like Wilhelm von Humboldt, Fichte, and Schleiermacher. Outstanding scholars in many subjects were invited to Berlin: the brothers Jacob and Wilhelm Grimm, founders of Germanic linguistics, the philologist Karl Lachmann, who studied Homeric and medieval epic, Leopold von Ranke, the leading German historian of the day, and Karl von Savigny, founder of the historical school in the study of law. The first large international congress of natural historians was held in Berlin in 1828.

The German universities, German philosophy, theology, philology, history, and law, and later also science, were the dominant influence on Lund University in the nineteenth century. It is a fact worthy of consideration that Jacob Grimm, Karl Lachmann, and Friedrich Schleiermacher visited Lund. A number of Lund scholars were in personal contact with their German colleagues and visited them on their travels south.

The chancellor of Lund University in the early nineteenth century was a man steeped in European culture, but rather of the French variety, Lars von Engeström. He was also foreign minister, and had previously been a diplomat.

It was in no small part due to him that the university became in his time an educational and cultural institute of note. 'He who fails to move forward with the century goes backwards' was one of his many exhortations to the university and its staff. It was on his personal initiative that many of the leading men of the university — among them Esaias Tegnér and Carl Adolph Agardh — were appointed to professorships. Yet his educational zeal had its negative side. The chairs were established without the provision of corresponding salaries. At best the newly appointed professor could continue to receive the salary he had earned in a previous inferior position in the university, while waiting for a superior or an older colleague to pass on.

Until the 1830s the university was a self-supporting institution, deriving its income solely from the university property and the tithes which had been assigned to it in the seventeenth century. A change came about when the Estates granted a new state allowance to the nation's two universities in 1830.

This reform had been preceded by government studies and proposals made by the Great Education Committee, also called the Genius Committee. It had selected some of the leading university brains in the country; from Lund came Tegnér, Agardh, and Lindfors. The statement of principle issued by the committee bore the unmistakable marks of the general view of culture and education typical of the Romantic Age. The final report declared that the universities were to be the centre of scientific training and the intellectual life of the nation. The universities must have a universal orientation, encompassing as far as possible the entire scope of human knowledge. The results of research in the various branches of learning were to be united into a harmonious whole; the dream of a *universitas scientiarum* was thus revived. It was by and large the same view of the role of the university which had been written into the programme of Berlin University at its foundation earlier in the century.

The Education Committee debated the topical issue of the contrast between the terms *utbildning* and *bildning*; both these words are usually rendered in English by 'education', but the former denotes practical, formal teaching, whereas the latter has a broader sense with connotations of learning, cultivation, and humanism. Tegnér declares in a letter of 1824 that the university has a twofold purpose: one scholarly and one practical. In the former role Tegnér sees the university as 'the sensorium not only of the Nation, but of the Age'. In the latter role he sees it as an institute for the training of public officials and clergy, as it was generally considered during the eighteenth century. If the two purposes collide, they cancel each other out. Tegnér's proposed solution to this conflict is to divide teaching in such a way as to give the assistant lecturers responsibility for practical training for qualifying examinations, allowing the professors to devote their time to pure scholarship. Both Tegnér and Agardh wished the university to continue to fulfil its duty of training students in criticism. As Agardh said: 'Academic inquiry must begin with scepsis and end with personal judgment, individual authority.'

The external framework

The external framework for the work of the university slowly changed in a number of stages during the nineteenth century. Although the number of students at the beginning of the century was restricted, with only about a hundred new admissions each year, and despite the modest size of the teaching staff, the university was cramped for space.

In the building to the south of the catheral which had formerly housed the cathedral chapter library, the Liberium, a fencing hall was appointed. It was Per Henrik Ling, the father of Swedish gymnastics, who directed the exercises here during his time as university fencing master between 1805 and 1813. He had also been to Copenhagen in the first years of the new century, and had there been caught up in the Scandinavian romantic revival.

The centre of academic life in Lund was, as before, Lundagård, which was still a walled enclosure where teachers and students strolled, and where the ceremonial academic processions passed between the cathedral and the university building. When student conscription was introduced, Lundagård became a drill ground. On the first of May it was the scene of festivities during which the students gathered under the fresh foliage and sang the old song which welcomed the month of May; in addition, in the early nineteenth century it was still possible to hear the 'Marseillaise' being sung in Lundagård. After the ceremony in Lundagård the students would continue their celebrations elsewhere, dancing in the Little Square and parading through the streets of the town, past professors' houses, where they would cry 'vivat', or occasionally 'pereat'.

Everyday life for the students was in general an uneventful existence in poorly furnished lodgings and student barracks. The latter often had picturesque names; one of them, Locus Peccatorum, called after a tragic murder, still stands, a half-timbered house preserved within the precincts of the Kulturen museum.

Student behaviour could still be rough: right up to the middle of the century the students still engaged in fisticuffs with apprentices and journeymen (contemptuously known because of their leather breeches as *brackor*, an epithet which came to be synonymous with 'philistines'). Opportunities for cultural diversions were very limited. Esaias Tegnér described Lund in 1826 as 'an academic peasant village, where one seldom sees any spectacle other than those improvised by students in the streets, or consistorial meetings within four walls.'

Food for the students was the simplest possible. Many young men from the province brought most of their food from their home villages; it could be preserved for months in food chests. Most of the students still came from homes in rural Scania. It is estimated that in the first decade of the nineteenth century some 26 per cent of the students were clergymen's sons and 19 per cent farmers' sons. By the 1860s the proportion of clergymen's sons had decreased while that of farmers' sons had increased.

Tegnér and Lundensian humanism

The two figures who dominate the Romantic Age in the history of Lund University are Esaias Tegnér and Carl Adolph Agardh. By a significant coincidence they both happened to matriculate on the same day, 4th October, 1799.

'Mr Tegnér is the sharpest and most erudite member of the student body.' This was the judgment of Anders Lidbeck, university librarian and professor of aesthetics, in a letter he wrote to the university chancellor in 1801, recommending the young Tegnér for the position of assistant librarian. At this time Tegnér was pursuing the study of philosophy, or as he put it himself, 'playing blind man's buff with Kant.' He was appointed lecturer in aesthetics in 1803. He also taught *artem poeticam* (the art of poetry) privately. It was in this art he was to achieve fame as one of the greatest poets of his age and of his country.

From 1812 Tegnér appears in the lecture catalogue as professor of Greek, although the list of his scholarly publications on classical philology was not impressive. For a little dissertation early in his career on the life of Anacreon he had Mathias Norberg as supervisor. It was the university chancellor who took the law into his own hands and had Tegnér appointed *graecae linguae professor*, without regard for the usual procedure of applications and nominations.

Of the ten years when he occupied this chair Tegnér writes in his autobiographical notes: 'Greek became a fashionable subject of study; and I can say without boasting that when I left, this literature was better known and respected at the university than when I came to it.' He himself saw Greek culture as the zenith of ancient history, and its humanism as an integral part of all human culture. The ideal of German neo-humanism proclaimed by Herder, Schiller, Goethe, and Humboldt was also Tegnér's.

His first lectures were on the topic of Homer's life and times; in later years he lectured on such subjects as Pindar's odes and Thucydides. The Homeric question had been raised by scholars of antiquity in Germany. Tegnér approached this topical issue from a historical standpoint and, like F. A. Wolf and Friedrich Schiller, he adhered to the view that the Homeric poems are products of 'an epic age', not of a single author.

Tegnér as a lecturer is described by a contemporary in his student memoirs. The account begins: 'First he construed word for word with extremely fine linguistic analysis and textual criticism.' After that, we are told,

> he elucidated the passage from the historical and antiquarian points of view, and finally gave a free rendering of it. Then no flight was too high for him, no allusion too refined, no combination too bold.

The classical cultural heritage which Tegnér passed on also included Plato's teaching on ideas in the form in which they had been renewed by contemporary German philosophers. It permeates his poetical-philosophical outlook in the poetry which he wrote after the romantic breakthrough around 1810. It is to be found in his interpretation of Christianity as expressed in his poems and sermons, both from his time as a prebendary during his years in Lund and after he became Bishop of Växjö in 1824.

As a member of the Education Committee he had occasion to review and to some extent revise his attitude to the role of the classical heritage for the modern age. He by no means rejected the rights of modern learning; he realized that the scientific revolution had already set its stamp on the new age.

Tegnér's role in the history of Lund University cannot be measured in terms of his teaching contribution or his published academic work. Yet through his poetry and his eloquence he brought lustre and renown to his university. In the memorial poems he wrote about the university teachers of his youth — Munthe, Fremling, Lidbeck, Lundblad, Norberg — he created a consciousness of tradition which the university had scarcely known before. His great academic speeches, all in Swedish, contained proclamations and watchwords which met with a sympathetic response from wide circles of people. With the art of the epigrammatist he formulated the credo of nineteenth-century humanism in the great epilogue in blank verse which he wrote for a graduation ceremony in the cathedral in 1820; at the same time he gave an ingenious and profound symbolic interpretation of the insignia of learning which are conferred as part of the graduation ceremony: the ring, the diploma, and the laurel wreath.

At a later conferring of masters' degrees in 1829, he elevated the ceremony in the cathedral to a symbolic dignity by inserting a half-improvised tribute to another poet, the Dane Adam Oehlenschläger. 'It was a sight for Italy, hardly for Scandinavia,' wrote his friend and colleague Agardh of this expression of Scandinavian unity.

It is scarcely an exaggeration to say that Tegnér created the Lundensian myth. Lund was for him 'Saxo's old town'; he thus forged links with medieval traditions of learning. He gave poetic status to the cult places of Lund's academic geography, Helgonabacken and Lundagård. In his poem 'Flyttningen' ('The Removal'), where he looks back on his many years in Lund, he says:

> Here is the earth where my soul has struck root. Like ivy it clings,
> Lundagård, to your arch, shouldered aloft on its piers.

Tegnér's local patriotism was not uncritical, however. Many of his comments show a complete lack of respect for things academic, an attitude similar to that found in eighteenth-century satires on scholarship, and one which to an extent formed a school of thought in later academic tradition in Lund. Yet Tegnér's tone of irony and criticism — as with many who followed in the Tegnérian tradition — is coupled with a sense of belonging to the local environment.

The circle of people for whom Tegnér displayed his rapier wit was known as *Härbärget*, after a former hostelry where the club met. This club saw the formation, according to Tegnér, of 'the essence of the opinions and thoughts which later were not without influence for the university. ... They played ball with ideas and flashes of wit which could well have deserved to become better known.' It was in this club that Tegnér read his latest poems, including the political and polemical works. Here they discussed literature and science, current events and fresh gossip; here they concocted academic intrigues — and Tegnér himself was a particularly gifted intriguer.

The academic social club of the Hostelry is an example of how intellectual life in a university town has always thrived best in small, confined circles. This sociologically interesting type of group is represented by many examples through the three centuries of Lund University's history.

For many years Tegnér lived in the one-storey house of which a few rooms are still preserved as a museum in Gråbrödersgatan. It was here he wrote *Frithiofs saga* (a verse tale based on an Icelandic saga, which achieved fame throughout Europe), 'Epilog' (the poem written for the graduation ceremony in 1820), and 'Mjältsjukan' ('Spleen', a poem written in a period of crisis). The

Statue of Esaias Tegnér, the poetic genius loci *of Lund, born in 1782, died 1846, professor of Greek 1812–1824. The statue, by C. G. Qvarnström, was erected to the south of the Academic Union building in 1853.*

house had two-and-a-half acres of pasture: the professor of Greek was also a farmer, owning merino sheep and good milch cows. His finances were nevertheless far from splendid. Like the other professors, Tegnér gave lodgings to young students and their tutors. Salaries were paid in grain: 150 barrels of rye and 150 of barley; this varied in value according to grain prices. Tegnér's statement that Lund was an academic peasant village was a correct description of the agrarian economy.

Tegnér's repute was spread across cultured Europe along with translations of his poems and speeches. In Lund he became a legend after his death. Seven years after his death his statue was unveiled outside the Academic Union in

1853. This was the first public statue in the town. A student tradition grew up the following decade; students assembled around the statue, bearing standards and torches and singing on 4th October, the date on which Tegnér was enrolled in the university. This Tegnér Commemoration was accompanied by a welcoming ceremony in which the newly matriculated students each year were received as members of the Academic Union with festivities and speeches. The Tegnér Commemoration with the welcoming ceremony was an annual event for over a century, not disappearing until the year of the student revolt, 1968, when so many traditions were swept away. Well into the twentieth century Tegnér has been held up as the foremost name of Lundensian humanism. It was his poem 'Det eviga' ('The Eternal') which was read on the wireless as 'Today's Poem' on 9th April, 1940, the day when Denmark and Norway were invaded by Hitler's troops.

Carl Adolph Agardh and botany

If Tegnér was the foremost humanist at Lund University, then Carl Adolph Agardh ranks as the prime talent in the natural sciences at the same time.

Agardh came to Lund a mere fourteen years old. During his childhood his interest in botany had been aroused by a vicar of the Linnaean type of the day. Agardh's teacher in Lund was Anders Jahan Retzius. In 1812 Agardh was appointed to the chair which included botany and practical economics; at the same time he became superintendent of the botanical gardens.

His extant diaries show how he developed in the direction of Romanticism. As a young man he read Jean Paul, Swedenborg, and Schelling's *Entwurf eines Systems der Naturphilosophie*. It was Schelling's fundamental beliefs which determined his view of creation, behind which he divined 'an idea, an infinite intelligence, which has ordered nature as one whole.' He saw nature as a harmonious, coherent scale including various degrees of perfection. In the vegetable kingdom too there was a hierarchy ascending to ever higher forms, from fungi and algae up to phanerogams.

At the same time, Agardh was an empiricist. He began by studying the lowest forms in the vegetable kingdom with a view to ordering them into a whole. In botany he made algae his special field. His systematic work with these has earned him the epithet 'the Linnaeus of algae'. In his *Systema Algarum* he laid the foundation for a branch of study, algalogy, which was a speciality of Lund well into this century.

He bequeathed his herbaria to the Botanical Institution; the collections have been increased by later generations of scholars. He himself made several research trips, the most important being to the Adriatic, accompanied by his young son, who was also to become a professor of botany and algalogist in his own time. On the journey home he met Schelling. It was in Schelling's company he believed he had observed in a microscope how an alga was transformed into a living animal, a sign of the unbroken chain of nature. To Schelling he dedicated a botanical textbook, which was also translated into German.

Agardh was one of those versatile but problematic geniuses in which the Romantic Age abounded. His wide range of interests had a divisive effect, somewhat reducing the influence of his undertakings. As a member of the 1825 Education Committee he made weighty contributions to the contemporary debate on the role and duties of the universities. He contested the utilitarian view of learning which had been maintained by previous generations; scholarship was to be pursued in freedom, independent of all external interests, regardless of the greater or lesser utility of the results. He was critical of the old-fashioned disputation system. In the modernization of the universities which he demanded he did not want to relinquish the classical heritage, but he championed the equal dignity of the sciences and the arts.

The professorship which Agardh held included practical economics alongside botany. He wrote an examination of the doctrines of political economy, in which he treated questions of the national debt and the monetary system.

Agardh was, among many other things, the driving force behind the creation of an institution specific to Lund, the Academic Union, an organization which includes both students and teachers. Together with a number of academics of the same age he formed a company which in 1830 bought a building east of Lundagård which became the first home of the Academic Union.

Agardh left Lund in 1835 to become Bishop of Karlstad. He is reckoned as one of the foremost teachers in the history of the university, and is famous also for his expository skill. In his lectures he dealt with general and special botany, and also with the new scientific discipline of plant physiology. Unlike Tegnér, who achieved fame and poetic imitators but scarcely any pupil of rank in his discipline, Agardh had many pupils who continued to pursue research in his subject.

One of them was Elias Fries, who ended his career as professor in Uppsala. Like Agardh, Fries represents the epoch's typical combination of empiricism and romantic speculation. One of Fries's masters was a German natural philosopher of the Schelling school, Lorentz Oken, regarded as a speculative predecessor of modern evolutionary theory. At the great congress of naturalists in Berlin in 1828 Fries met this imaginative scholar in person. Oken's ideas on the plan of creation were followed by Fries in his most important work on botanical classification, *Systema Mycologicum*, published in Lund and Greifswald. He here summarizes in Latin his research on fungi for the benefit of an international audience.

Elias Fries gradually distanced himself from the excessive speculativeness of natural philosophy. In his next work, a survey of the lichens of Europe, there are no longer any quotations from the romantic natural philosophers whom he had so often cited in previous writings. Yet he held as faithfully as his master to the basic view of a divine principle manifested in the forms of nature, a view which was common to the whole generation of romantic scholars.

Theology and the romantic breakthrough

Romanticism penetrated the various faculties of scholarly society in Lund at varying speeds. The change came relatively late to the theological faculty, where orthodoxy and rationalism long reigned supreme.

For decades to come the old regulations continued to require students of law, medicine, or philosophy to sit a preliminary examination in theology. A large part of the teaching and examination in the faculty was consequently on a very elementary level.

A few teachers representing the sententious Enlightenment view of Christianity continued to haunt the first decades of the nineteenth century. One of them, Christian Wåhlin, was and still is well known as the subject of mercilessly revealing anecdotes. But a new scientific spirit was on its way.

In theology too the new ideas came from Germany, mainly from Kant, but also from Schleiermacher. The latter drew a distinct boundary between the sphere of religion on the one hand, and that of knowledge and morality on the other. Religion was for him conveyed through immediate attitudes and feelings. Perceived as a part of empirical reality, religious belief became an independent sphere susceptible to objective analysis and description. The eighteenth-century ambition to prove the existence of God by logical argument was definitively abandoned.

Proceeding directly from this standpoint of Schleiermacher's, the leading Lundensian theologians maintained the position of theology as a branch of scholarship equal in status to other disciplines. Their manifesto was a periodical started in 1828, *Theologisk Quartalskrift*, a publication which was to be epoch-making for Swedish theology. The initiative was taken by Henrik Reuterdahl.

As a young man Reuterdahl had been enraptured by Schleiermacher's *Reden über die Religion* and his major work, the dogmatic *Der christliche Glaube*. This made him immune to the excesses of rationalism, the old orthodoxy, and the Hegelian attempt to ensnare religion in the system of reason.

One morning in 1833, when Reuterdahl had just returned home from the cathedral, an unknown man was waiting for him in his hall. 'A little hunch-backed old man with a big head, clear, light eyes, and the features of a man of genius.' The stranger presented himself with the words: 'Ich bin Professor Schleiermacher aus Berlin.' Reuterdahl continues his account thus: 'I do not know of any visit which could have made a deeper or more powerful impression on me. Schleiermacher was still for me the greatest theologian, the most convincing philosopher, the man who had solved all the most important questions of life and thought in the most correct and incontrovertible way.' It was a symbolic moment in the history of Lundensian theology. The meeting had been arranged by Esaias Tegnér, who had visited Schleiermacher in Berlin during a trip to Germany and had given him Reuterdahl's address.

Reuterdahl spent thirty years on his four-volume work *Svenska kyrkans historia*, which described the ecclesiastical history of Sweden up to the Reformation. It was a pioneering work for the time, particularly in its critical use of the sources, in deliberate contrast to Hegelian constructions of history. His final appointment was as Archbishop of Uppsala, where he grew more conservative both politically and religiously than he was during his years in Lund or during the European tour which had brought him into contact with most of the leading theologians of his age.

Reuterdahl's friend from youth, Johan Henrik Thomander, differed from him diametrically in both temperament and later on also in ideology. In his early years Thomander had devoted his time to literature, chiefly as a translator. He published renderings of Aristophanes and Byron, and translated no less than five plays of Shakespeare into Swedish.

'They are using the devil's own powers to win me over to theology, a subject scarcely to my taste,' wrote Thomander as a young student. Yet once he had entered the theological faculty as a professor, first in pastoral theology, later in dogmatics, he made significant contributions to the subject.

He was a dominant figure in the Lund of his day, with a powerful ability to inspire and dazzle, but also to scandalize. Agardh wrote the following ambivalent reference for him when he was up for consideration for the position of dean of the cathedral:

Thomander is far superior [to the other candidates], superior by virtue of his healthy nature, his sound body, his lively manner, his inventiveness, his wit, his knowledge of modern literature, his ability to come forth when it counts, his audacity, his boldness, his aplomb, his way of making himself important and all others insignificant. He is capable in everything, as a courtier, a minor poet, a statesman, a littérateur, a translator, a reviewer, a lawyer, a priest, a professor, so why not also as a dean?

His liberalism, together with his wit and brilliance as a speaker, won him popularity among the student generation of the 1830s. When the first chairman had to be selected for the newly founded Academic Union, the choice was Thomander. He later succeeded his former friend and later adversary Reuterdahl as Bishop of Lund and vice-chancellor of the university. His powerful voice was once again heard in the cathedral, where he was one of the most eloquent and distinguished preachers of his day.

After the group behind the *Theologisk Quartalskrift* with its broad perspective and its defence of scholarly freedom, there followed a new generation, a theological faculty with a firmer bearing and stricter religious observance. These were spokesmen for the new high church, champions of the monopoly of the state church and upholders of the priestly office, who saw the church as an institute for salvation.

In their case too the influences came from Germany. The right flank of Hegelianism had been taken over by a speculative theology of a conservative character. The neo-Lutheran theologian Theodor Kliefoth of Mecklenburg provided the high-church theologians of Lund with the principles which they proclaimed in the periodical started in 1855, *Svensk kyrkotidning*. Their dependence on the German theologian led to the punning accusation that the faculty did not stand on its own *foot* but on Klie*foth*.

An indication of a more radical strain of theological thought in Germany of the 1830s came from the left flank of Hegelianism, with David Friedrich Strauss and his book on the life of Jesus. Strauss saw the gospels not as accounts of historical events but as the creations of a mythical imagination. His book aroused controversy in Sweden, as elsewhere. One of the professors in the high-church faculty in Lund, H.M. Melin, criticized it heavily in a series of lectures on the life of Christ which he later issued as a book.

The historical school of law

The early years of the nineteenth century gave a new lease of life to the faculty of law. This was primarily due to Johan Holmbergsson. The new examinations statute of 1815 was essentially his work. It attached great importance to the history of law. This was, again, under the influence of the German school of legal historians; men like Adam Müller and the Berlin professor Karl von Savigny had elaborated a view of legal philosophy which was diametrically opposed to the ideas of natural law. Instead of seeing law as something with a foundation in human nature, they regarded the legal order as a national development. Laws are thus viewed as the bequest of previous centuries, the essence of national history. The state is seen through the historical philosophy of the Romantics.

Carl Johan Schlyter was the foremost spokesman of the historical school of law in Lund. He followed Savigny in his dissertation on the study of the history of law, published in 1835. The school attached central importance to the study of the nation's oldest extant legal texts, which were deemed important also for modern legislation.

The need for a critical edition of the medieval Swedish laws was expressed by a committee which had the task of revising the laws of 1734. Schlyter himself sat on the committee. His great plan involved the comparison of all the existing printed and unprinted legal texts from the Middle Ages. The documents to be compared amounted in the case of some laws to a hundred; every variant reading had to be recorded. The edition of the laws fills twelve large volumes which appeared over a period of forty-two years, the last in 1869. Besides the texts, there are descriptions of the manuscripts and details of the ages and sources of the laws.

The publication of the old laws did not have the importance which Schlyter had envisaged for concrete legislation. It is mostly as a textual scholar that he is remembered. To establish the relationships of the various manuscripts, Schlyter drew up a stemma, a sort of family tree. His tree diagram of 1827, constructed on the basis of errors common to more than one manuscript, is considered the first of its kind in the history of philology. Before the German medievalists he had arrived at the approach usually known as Lachmann's method.

Schlyter was already renowned in his lifetime for his scholarship. His work was also justly appreciated by German scholars in the history of law, with their interest in the legal monuments of the early Germanic peoples.

Medicine in Lund — practitioners and romantics

Romantic philosophy also left its mark on the natural sciences and medicine. The mechanistic outlook of the Leiden doctor Boerhaave and his disciples provoked a reaction from a number of biologists and physicians at the end of the eighteenth century. They believed in dynamism and vitality, returning to the idea of a secret life force, *vis vitalis*, as the ultimate basis of all forms of life. Health and disease, life and death were put into a cosmic context by the medical scholars of the Romantic Age.

Students of medicine in Lund in the early nineteenth century were thoroughly familiar with the speculative theories. This is evident from lecture programmes, where we find subjects like 'the properties of *vis vitalis* and the extended sphere of influence', 'the relationship of the organism to the universe and its separate parts', 'lunar influence on the human body', 'the life force and electricity as identical.' Lund also had its advocates of animal magnetism, Doctor Mesmer's theory of the universal fluid which could be transferred to a patient through the doctor's hands. However, the romantic theories of medicine also met criticism from various quarters. One of the leading scholars in the Lund faculty characterized this philosophy of nature as 'medicine elevated on the stilts of Idealism, with no stable footing'.

Most of the medical scholars of the nineteenth century were also practising doctors. All four professors in the faculty had studied abroad. While on a study tour of Europe, Johan Henrik Engelhart had met William Cullen, the foremost man in the Edinburgh school. Engelhart became a member of an English medical society and, back in Sweden, he later became physician to the royal household.

The other three professors in the Lund faculty had all studied in Copenhagen, where medicine was at a high standard, and where there was a well developed hospital. The professor of anatomy, Arvid Florman, was duly warned in Copenhagen not to indulge in 'speculative reasoning'. He introduced the study of comparative anatomy, wrote textbooks in the subject, and worked assiduously on autopsies in the anatomical theatre of the Orangerie. Florman was an outstanding human pathologist, as well as Sweden's first anthropologist.

Eberhard Zacharias Munck av Rosenschöld occupied the chair of theoretical medicine. In his lectures he treated such widely different topics as Gall's phrenological work *Cranioscopie*, John Brown's homeopathy, towards which he was critical, and the animal magnetism which was so celebrated at the time. In the circle of Danish scholars where he liked to move he was attracted by a discovery made by the Englishman Edward Jenner in 1796, which made it possible to vaccinate against smallpox using cowpox. Rosenschöld carried out the first vaccination in Sweden, and issued popular pamphlets campaigning for smallpox innoculation.

During the eighteenth century there had been little connection between medical teaching and clinical practice. On the initiative of the university chancellor, Engeström, an *Institutum Clinicum* was established, beginning its work in 1813. Clinical lectures were held here, giving medical students the practical experience of doing rounds, diagnosing and treating patients. For higher education in surgery there were as yet only the opportunities afforded by the Medico-Chirurgical Institute in Stockholm, later the Royal Caroline Institute. This meant in practice that those who desired full competence as state or civil physicians had to study both at the university in Lund and in the capital.

In the mid-1820s the hospital consisted of three buildings: the hospital building itself, a newly erected maternity clinic, and a newly built sanatorium for the treatment of venereal disease. The latter building, completed in 1824, still stands on the corner of Sandgatan and Paradisgatan, the oldest surviving building from the old hospital. Having long been used as an out-patients' department, it has undergone a symbolic transformation to become an administration building today.

Antiquarians and philologists

In the faculty of philosophy, where Tegnér and Agardh were the big names, and the spirit of Romanticism was in the air, there were still many remains of the sober empiricism and collecting passion of the eighteenth century. In the field of history, the romantic speculation which was noticeable in Uppsala was less evident in Lund. On the other hand, interest in Nordic antiquity was equally keen in both universities. It is customary to speak of a 'Nordic Renaissance' in the late eighteenth century and the early nineteenth. This found expression in research, poetry, and art. The outstanding poetic document of this revival is Tegnér's *Frithiofs saga* (which has been translated into the major European languages, fifteen times into English). The scholarly achievements were partly in the field of archaeology, partly in philology, in the study of the Old Norse sagas and poetry. A representative of both these interests in Lund was Nils Henrik Sjöborg.

Sjöborg's inspiration came both from Denmark and from Germany. He had studied at the Arnemagnaean collection of manuscripts in Copenhagen; he

Conferring of degrees in the cathedral. The wreath girls in white sit on the chancel steps.

edited Icelandic poems, *Rígsmál* and *Loðbrókar-Qviða*, with text and translation. He further promoted the study of Icelandic with a Latin grammar of that language. His main work, however, was in Scandinavian archaeology, as a typical representative of this age of collectors and topographers.

His name is also associated with the history of Lundensian graduation ceremonies. In 1811, when Sjöborg himself was conferring the degrees, he introduced the charming custom of the 'wreath girls'. These were originally nine in number, to symbolize the nine muses; they were accompanied by a boy in a white cloak, representing Apollo. This rococo-classical feature has been Sjöborg's lasting bequest to the academic cermonials, long unique for Lund.

That it was but a short step from the classics to Nordic studies in Lund at this time is further demonstrated by the career of a scholar who for a number of years deputized as professor of history, but whose final position was as professor of Roman oratory and poetry. His name was Anders Otto Lindfors.

He studied Icelandic in Copenhagen under one of the pioneer figures of the Nordic Renaissance, the linguist Rasmus Rask. His most important work, however was done in Latin, and his Latin-Swedish dictionary made him one of Lund's first lexicographers.

Latin was still a compulsory language for all students at the university, and Old Icelandic had become a fashionable subject. The teaching of the three main languages of Europe had been in the hands of foreign language masters from the earliest days of the university. A sign of the start of the decline of Latin as the sole language of scholarship is the chair of French, German, and English which Mathias Norberg donated to the university in 1811. In his donation charter he wrote: 'If anything is necessary for a place of higher education, it is certainly an enlightened teacher of the living languages.' The first occupant of the chair was, due to an unfortunate nepotistic appointment, an ignoramus. A generation was to pass before the study of modern European linguistics reached a satisfactory level.

The slow progress of the natural sciences

Physics, chemistry, and mathematics languished in obscurity during the Romantic Age in the early nineteenth century. It was only through a slow differentiation process that the separate subjects achieved anything like an independent position. Mathematics obtained its own chair in 1812. Two decades later a professorship in physics was established by royal decree; physics had previously been part of astronomy for many years. In the days of Anders Jahan Retzius, chemistry had been included in natural history along with zoology, botany, and mineralogy. In the 1830s a new professorship was created for chemstry and mineralogy, a combination which lasted until the start of the twentieth century.

Electricity had become the focus of study in physics in the middle of the eighteenth century. At this time an electricity machine and an early version of the famous Leiden jar were added to the instrument chamber of the university.

Towards the end of the eighteenth century a new era in the history of physics was inaugurated by the discoveries of Galvani and Volta in the field of electrodynamics. It is assumed that galvanic current was demonstrated on the occasion when the new king, Gustav IV Adolf, together with Queen Fredrika visited Lund in September 1801.

The last professor to combine the subjects of physics and astronomy was Jonas Brag, who had studied in Copenhagen under Ørsted, the great physicist who had immersed himself in the romantic philosophy of nature of Friedrich Schelling and Henrik Steffens.

The first professor of physics as an independent subject was Adam Wilhelm Ekelund, who represented the sober empirical trend of a future period. When he was appointed to the new position in 1839, he was granted leave of absence to acquire the modern apparatus needed to put the resources of the institute on an equal footing with those of foreign universities. A representative collection of apparatus for experiments in electromagnetism, electrostatics, acoustics, optics, and heat was purchased from instrument makers in Paris. The collection which was handed over to the university in 1840 also included the equipment necessary for Daguerre's photographic process.

Like physics, chemistry had been developed into an empirical science from the early nineteenth century. Work of fundamental importance had been carried out by a Swede, Jöns Jacob Berzelius, professor at the Caroline Institute in Stockholm. It was he who drew up the first table of atomic weights and introduced a uniform nomenclature to the subject. From the 1860s a Lundensian chemist, Christian Wilhelm Blomstrand, continued and developed the Berzelian tradition, producing excellent work, including a book entitled *Die Chemie der Jetztzeit* in 1869. He sought to go beyond empirical facts to arrive at a synthesis. He was still an authority at the time when August Strindberg was teaching himself the fundamentals of science.

Blomstrand was known for his tireless energy. For days on end he could start work at six o'clock in the morning and carry on until midnight. Dressed in a long nightshirt which bore the marks of his laboratory work, with a pipe constantly puffing in his mouth, he became known for his eccentricity — the isolated small town atmosphere of the nineteenth century fostered such eccentric professors. As a lecturer Blomstrand had a sonorous voice; when he dropped his voice he always sounded tearful, so the students would say: 'Oh dear, Blomstrand is crying because the atoms are too small.'

A polymath in the natural sciences

One of the most versatile and original representatives of scholarship in natural history in Lund was Sven Nilsson, professor of the subject from 1832 to 1856. He pursued his research long into his emeritus years, and did not die until 1883.

He made great contributions to three fields: zoology, geology, and archaeology. He appears to have been totally unaffected by the idealistic speculation of romantic natural philosophy. He was a true empiricist by nature, as he expressed in the maxim: 'Only naked truth is valid currency.'

He came to Lund for the same purpose as many farmers' sons: to become a clergyman. At the psychological moment Retzius offered him a position as lecturer in natural history and research assistant at the museum of natural history. He later enriched these collections with discoveries in peat bogs of the relics of a lost animal world, among them aurochs and bison skeletons.

Botany had been dominant since the days of Linnaeus, whereas zoology was at this time a relatively new subject. Sven Nilsson continued his studies in zoology, anatomy, and mineralogy at Copenhagen, where he published the two volumes of his *Ornithologia Svecica*, a book which won acclaim from foreign scholars in Germany and Holland. A Swedish translation of the Latin original appeared as part of his classical work on Scandinavian fauna. Other parts covered mammals, amphibians (which at this time also included reptiles), and fish. This work made him the founder of modern Swedish faunology.

The professor of natural history was also responsible for geology in these days. Sven Nilsson's study of fossil animals and plants in coal formations and deposits culminated in his work *Petrificata Suecana* in 1827. Finds of subfossil mammals in the peat bogs of Scania led him to launch the then epoch-making theory that Scania had once been part of the European continent and that its fauna had migrated there from the south. At the first congress of natural history in Gothenburg in 1839 he spoke about a problem of general geology, the alternating rise and fall of the earth's surface in Southern Sweden. In a series of lectures in Stockholm in the 1840s he presented a summary of his views on the general geological structure of Scandinavia.

One of Sven Nilsson's pupils, Otto Torell, studied glacial geology with more comprehensive empirical material and a more reliable methodology. On research trips to the Alps, Iceland, Spitzbergen, Greenland, and Northern Finnmark he made detailed investigations of glacial formations, which led to the theory of the great ice age. When Torell was appointed in 1866 to an extraordinary professorship in Lund — the subject combination now being zoology and geology — a more independent position was assigned to geology. He is the first scholar who can legitimately be called a professional geologist.

Sven Nilsson had begun collecting antiquities already in his youth. His studies of the history of fishing and hunting drew his attention to the appearance of the various tools. He compared fishing and hunting tools of stone and bone from Scandinavian antiquity with similar tools used by the natives of North America and Australia. He took the comparative method which had begun to be used in anatomy and applied it to anthroplogy. The result was the great work *Skandinaviska Nordens Ur-invånare* (translated as *The Primitive Inhabitants of Scandinavia*), an attempt at a comparative ethnography and a contribution to the cultural history of the human race.

Sven Nilsson's work links the more static eighteenth-century view of science typified by Retzius with the historical, evolutionary perspective of the nineteenth century. He has also been regarded as a pioneer in social science; in the 1830s he analysed the development of human societies, classifying them into four categories, based not on technological progress but on economic development. Ideas of progress were stimulated afresh by the study of primitive peoples.

He shows the same evolutionary perspective in his research on Nordic antiquity. He adopted the three-period system of Stone Age, Bronze Age, and Iron Age (his immediate source being his Danish colleague C.J. Thomsen). Nilsson envisaged that the three ages had been introduced by different peoples. His ideas about the Bronze Age achieved particular fame and controversy. Using the evidence of the ornamentation of bronze objects, he tried to prove that a Phoenician tribe had brought the Bronze Age to Scandinavia by a sea route. The most common decorative motif, the spiral, reminded him of weapons from the Homeric Age. These and other of Sven Nilsson's bolder theories have been abandoned by later scholars with a greater knowledge of the diffusion of cultural and utility objects.

His work attracted considerable attention abroad; several of his books were translated into the three main European languages. One of his publications is still preserved in Charles Darwin's library. He corresponded with Darwin, who was at this time working on *The Descent of Man*. The English naturalist built the jigsaw puzzle of his theory with the help of some pieces from Sven Nilsson.

Nilsson had a wide network of contacts both inside and outside Scandinavia. Three hundred of the eight hundred correspondents in his collection of letters are foreigners. There are many letters from his Danish colleague Thomsen. A few come from the English geologist Charles Lyell, who visited Nilsson in Lund when he was studying land elevation in Sweden. Also extant are some thirty letters from Sir John Lubbock, who published the English edition of Nilsson's *The Primitive Inhabitants of Scandinavia*.

He fostered these scholarly contacts by participating in many of the international congresses which were such an important new feature of nineteenth-century learning. Along with a number of other Swedish scholars he attended the great gathering of natural historians in Berlin, so brilliantly conducted by Alexander von Humboldt. He went to the English natural history conferences in Bristol, Oxford, and Bath; he helped to inaugurate similar conferences in Scandinavia, and he was a regular guest at archaeological congresses, including that in Paris in 1867. Hardly anyone in his generation cultivated foreign connections to the same extent as Sven Nilsson.

Yet his roots were in Lund. He was self-assured as a professor, quite the despot, quick to disagree with his colleagues. Many envied and resented him, including Esaias Tegnér, who described him in the following highly ironic tone: 'The man is famous for his ability to scale fish and feel hens, all on a purely scientific basis.'

Ever since Anders Jahan Retzius had as a research assistant lectured on the economic significance and utility of insects, entomology had had its place in zoological research in Lund. During the nineteenth century it was represented by a range of scholars, each with his own specialist group or groups of insects: both C.A. Fallén and his successor J.W. Zetterstedt wrote about the two-winged order, the Diptera. Carl Gustaf Thomson catalogued 2,375 insects new to the Swedish fauna, wrote ten volumes on Coleoptera (beetles), five volumes on Hymenoptera (the order which includes ant, bees, and wasps), and a twenty-two-volume *Opuscula Entomologica*.

The entomological museum which was created in Lund thanks to the work of new generations of scholars contains Sweden's largest insect collection. Not until 1949 did Lund get its first professorship in entomology. When the first occupant — Carl H. Lindroth – left the chair, the position was redesignated as a professorship in systematic zoology.

Liberalism and Scandinavianism

Memoirs of Lund in the early days of the nineteenth century are dominated by the powerful scholarly personages. In the 1830s and 1840s the contemporary reminiscences are by contrast full of a young student generation with a new self-assurance and a group identity, even though they were not yet formally organized into a student union. The students represent a more or less conscious idea of youth as a creative force and an agent of progress. Here, as in many places in Europe, the romantic spirit of a young generation went along with or developed into liberalism.

The students were now active in the creation of new institutions and new traditions. From the first decades of the university's existence, the student nations had played an important role, with patriarchal relations between the inspectors of each nation and the newly enrolled members. The nations survived, but from 1830 they were autonomous subdivisions of the Academic Union, which included all the students in all the nations. This body had as its closest model the Student Union in Copenhagen, but with the important difference that in Lund the academic dons were also a part of the new corporation.

A building in Sandgatan had been bought, and this was where the students of Lund for the first time found a home of their own. Rooms were appointed within its walls for club activities of great diversity. The social division had the duty of organizing lectures and discussions, musical soirées and theatrical entertainments. Another division was the Atheneum, a literary society and reading room which subscribed to Swedish and foreign newspapers and periodicals of political and general cultural interest. A third division, known as the Convictorium, was a club where students could eat together.

The Academic Union gave students opportunities for socializing, club work, discussions, political activity, and a varied cultural life outside the tight bounds of their formal studies. Singing was an important new activity, with the organization of a choral society performing concerts. After the Lund Students' Song Club, founded early in the 1830s, had acquired Otto Lindblad as conductor, the repertoire was dominated by his compositions. Prince Gustaf's Student Song — beginning with the words *Sjungom studentens lyckliga dag* — is still today an essential part of May Day celebrations; the song caught on shortly after the middle of the century.

New winds were blowing in Europe after the calm and political reaction of the Romantic Age. The year 1830 saw the July revolution in France and the Polish uprising. Sympathy for the Polish freedom fighters was translated into action when three young medical students volunteered as field surgeons.

On repeated occasions during the 1830s and 1840s the students of Lund demonstrated their sympathies for liberal reforms at home. In the more conservative Uppsala, where the proportion of nobility in the student body was higher, the Lund students gained the reputation of being 'free-thinking and bold', and more democratic in their social intercourse.

These decades also marked the culmination of student enthusiasm for national liberalism with its Scandinavianism. The actual origin of the movement was in Denmark, where there was a general aspiration to unite all the Nordic countries in a political federation which would ward off the German military threat to Schleswig. The movement gained ground among the young generations of students. When the sound froze in the winter of 1838, students from Lund and Copenhagen took the opportunity to exchange visits. Contacts between the two student bodies continued the following decades on a larger scale and with a more permanent organization. In 1843 a large Pan-Scandinavian meeting was held in Uppsala, with participants from all the Nordic countries. In 1845 both Lund and Copenhagen were the scene of youthful demonstrations of Scandinavianism; these occasions represent the culmination of the student movement. It was also at this time that the white cap was first worn as a student emblem.

The atmosphere of Scandinavianism inspired the young poets of the day. C.W. Strandberg appeared at a student meeting in Lund with a rousing plea for liberty for Finland; the country which had for so long been a Swedish possession had been lost in the war of 1808–1809 and was now under Russian domination. One of the Danish poets who was profoundly affected by the mood of Scandinavianism was Hans Christian Andersen. He was applauded by the students when he wrote in a student publication following a visit to Lund:

> On fells, in woods, and by the ocean blue
> I shout with joy: 'I am a Nordic true!'

The first Academic Union building. Political debate

In the decades which followed, the scene of many demonstrations of Nordic, particularly Swedish–Danish, solidarity was the redbrick fortress of the Academic Union. On 14th May, 1851, the flags were hoisted to the top of the towers as a sign that the new union building was inaugurated. Since then it has often been extended, rebuilt, and restored, but it has remained the centre of student life for over a century, with discussions, lectures, music, and drama. A festive student calendar with fixed rituals took shape. Two festive days were for a long time specific to Lund. One was the fourth of October, when the newly enrolled 'novices' were welcomed into the Academic Union. The other was — and still is — the first of May, the day when students put on 'the white cap' for the first time in the year, and accompanied by banners and song call on the rector on the steps of the University Building.

The Pan-Scandinavian student movement, which had been a feature of university life from the 1840s, lost its political credibility with the German attack on Denmark in the war of 1863–1864. Only a few Lund students volunteered to fight for the Danish cause. The débâcle of Scandinavianism led students to search for new forms for co-operation between Sweden and Denmark, not through political measures but through cultural activity. One result of this was the foundation of the Oehlenschläger-Tegnér Scholarship

Fund, which has given and continues to give students the opportunity to study at other Nordic universities. This gesture of Scandinavianism was to be of decisive importance for the generation of scholars who gave Lund University its profile in the closing years of the nineteenth century.

The liberal wave which had stimulated the leading forces in the student union in the 1830s and 1840s slowly ebbed away. The same student union which had been praised — or scorned — for its free-thinking had the reputation a few decades later of being fiercely reactionary. When it was suggested that the 1865 liberal representation reform — when the assembly of the four estates was replaced by a bicameral parliament — be celebrated with an illumination, the proposal was rejected by 98 votes to 65.

But the new age and the new nation were not to be stopped. The old society of the estates was breaking up. Industrialism and the labour movement were gaining ground even in agrarian Sweden, hand in hand with the new technology. Sweden's first locomotive chugged on its maiden journey on the southern main line between Lund and Malmö in 1856, festively adorned for the occasion. Despite the misgivings of a few conservative professors, it was the railway which brought the provincial town of Lund into closer contact with Denmark and the continent, and eased the communication of ideas. For over a century Lund has been a natural stopping place for foreign academics visiting Sweden. Throughout the nineteenth century it was also a tradition that passing celebrities, such as Ibsen and Strindberg, were honoured by student welcomes on the platform of Lund Central Station.

Although liberalism declined in the 1860s, the Pan-Scandinavian ideal survived. It had its Indian summer in the 1870s. A neo-Nordic revival was supported by influential poets and dramatists in Sweden and Norway. Old Norse literature, especially Icelandic, was studied with renewed intensity. An educational movement combining Christian and Nordic idealism was started in Denmark by N.F. Grundtvig, from where it spread to Sweden, leading to the creation of the first so-called folk high school, Hvilan, a few miles south of Lund. It was founded in intimate contact with Lund University, from where leading teachers were drawn.

New statutes, new examinations

From the middle of the nineteenth century there was a modernization of the university constitution, its working forms and its examinations system. New statutes were issued in 1852 for Uppsala and Lund together, and in the following year a new examinations statute. The new rules show many features of the liberal view of society, learning, and culture.

It was stipulated that teaching should not be limited solely to the requirements of examinations, but instead have as its goal the independent scholarly development of the students. As regards lectures: 'Each teacher is otherwise free to arrange his lectures and his teaching in such a way as he finds appropriate to the subject and suited to the purpose of spreading true enlightenment.' Paragraph 117 of the 1852 statutes has been called the Magna Charta of Swedish academic teaching. It was in force for a century, guaranteeing that the teaching of every subject would be free from influence from both above and below. The provision disappeared in a different economic and educational climate, in 1956, although no one at first appeared to have noticed anything significant about the loss of this aspect of academic freedom.

Nineteenth-century lectures were free in another sense: student attendance was not compulsory. Compulsory teaching tied to courses is an invention of a later age. The mentality behind the 1852 statutes corresponds well with what the Lund Consistory expressed in a statement of its own, that the university should be 'a sanctuary for the sciences', and that the duty of the university teacher was to 'cultivate with all zeal the individual branches of scholarship to bring them to their highest possible perfection'. In agreement with this is another paragraph in the new statutes, which states that only formal academic qualifications can be taken into consideration when appointing new teachers. This was a step towards professionalism and specialization. Entirely in line with the new age's more rigorous view of scholarship, documented through published work, was the foundation of the series Acta Universitatis Lundensis, which first appeared in 1864.

The statutes had special provisions to regulate the election of the university chancellor, from now on responsible for both universities. The forms whereby the rector was elected were likewise regulated. At the same time the university court, which had been empowered to try university officials, their families, and the students, was abolished. Only isolated disciplinary cases remained within the jurisdiction of the university. In this way the university people, who had once formed a distinct and independent guild with privileges similar to those of the church, were integrated into the new society.

Further new regulations came in the statutes of 1876. One such concerned the election of a committee of experts — three professors — to assess candidates for professorial appointments. Their duty was to propose three names to fill a vacant chair, with a detailed written report stating the reasons for the choice. This further established the need for documented proof of scholarly ability in the individual subjects. The committee of experts in this form existed for a hundred years. It survived until a new era of cultural politics, when the three experts were replaced by three 'special members' of a committee, with less weight attached to their opinions.

A number of changes reshaped the examinations system in the course of the nineteenth century. An examinations statute of 1853 abolished the preliminary examination in theology, which had long been compulsory for all those wishing to take a master's or a doctor's degree in other faculties. The disappearance of the theological preliminary was a symbolic change, indicating that the faculty of theology could no longer be considered to have a superior position in the university system. Another sign of secularization was the loss in the 1850s of the regulation concerning confessional orthodoxy which had previously been on the statute book.

The superior role of theology was transferred to philosophy. It was established in 1853 that studies in theology, law, and medicine should be preceded by a new preliminary examination — a test by the philosophical faculty. The same statute introduced a new Bachelor of Arts examination

In 1870 the new examination regulations were revised. The comprehensive bachelor's degree was replaced by two degrees: a bachelorship (*filosofie kandidat*) and a licentiate (*filosofie licentiat*). The former was supposed, according to the Lund syllabus of the same year, to provide 'a general foundation in scholarly study, with the emphasis on the humanities, which is the chief goal of the faculty; it is thus essentially a preparatory examination for the licentiate.' The predominantly scholarly purpose of the university was thereby formulated once again.

The bachelor's examination required both arts and science subjects — the division into what has been called 'the two cultures' of the arts and sciences had not yet taken place. But the division was indirectly acknowledged in the statutes of 1876, when the sciences were given a more independent position. The philosophy faculty was then divided into two sections, the humanities and the natural sciences. This division survived until 1956, when the two sections became independent faculties.

The new licentiate examination of the 1870 statutes included three subjects. In one of these the student had to write a dissertation. For the doctor's degree the dissertation had to be printed, although it was still of modest format. When it was to be publicly defended, two opponents were appointed. There also arose the unofficial institution of the third opponent with the delicate task of making fun of the dissertation, the author, and to an extent also mocking the gravity of the whole ceremony. The forms of the doctor's dissertation and the disputation remained largely unchanged for almost a century.

It was stipulated that dissertations should be written either in Swedish or in one of the major European languages; only in the classical disciplines was it still possible to write a thesis in Latin. The final retreat of Latin at the university was thus complete. Latin had been used up to 1866 for the lecture catalogue, entitled *Index Scholarum*, with details of all teaching by professors, lecturers, and assistant lecturers. In the autumn term of 1866 there appeared for the first time a Swedish edition alongside the Latin. After a few years the lecture list was printed only in Swedish, a sign of changing times.

After all the reforms there remained a single ceremony of medieval origin: the passage rite which is the doctors' graduation ceremony, with the conferring of the old insignia of learning. A survival to the present day are the magic formulas spoken in the old language of scholarship and the church, Latin, an echo of an ancient culture. The Latin prayer with which the ceremony ends, read in the cathedral by the Bishop of Lund, is also a historical relic from a former age. It preserves a link with the time when the bishop of the diocese was the vice-chancellor of the university, when Latin was the official language of the university, and when the confession of pure Lutheran orthodoxy was a part of the obligatory student oath and the oath of office sworn by every professor when he took up his appointment.

C. G. Brunius and the dream of the Middle Ages

In the middle of the century the face of Lund was changing.

The cathedral was restored by Carl Georg Brunius, Tegnér's successor in the chair of Greek. With a stonemason's tools in his hands, he himself mounted the scaffolds to supervise every detail of the work; there is a well-known anecdote about the wording of his visiting card: 'can be found in the cathedral every day except Sunday'.

Brunius left his mark not just on the restoration of the cathedral. He was also commissioned to rebuild the old university building in Lundagård. Brunius believed to the very last that this was a medieval building, identical with the ancient bishop's castle. He rescued a doorway with Romanesque columns from a transverse wall which had been removed from the cathedral, and had it moved to form the entrance to the scene of academic ceremonials at this time, the Caroline Hall. There is a profound historical and symbolic significance in the fact that even today we still enter one of the oldest halls of the university through

*Jacob Erlansen's door-
way, which C. G. Bru-
nius had removed from
the cathedral to the
Lundagård building
which he restored. It is
now the entrance to the
Caroline Hall.*

a church door. Brunius's historical mistake regarding the house in Lundagård
led him to erect a number of new buildings in the same supposed medieval
Romanesque style, including the Historical Museum and the Bishop's Palace.
Medieval romanticism survives in these examples of Lundensian architecture.

Parallel to his practical work on the restoration of the cathedral, Brunius
finished the manuscript of his monograph *Nordens äldsta metropolitankyrka*,
a historical and architectural account of Lund cathedral, the first monograph
on a Scandinavian church to concentrate on the history of its art and

architecture. Brunius compares the testimony of written sources with what he himself observed and deduced from a study of walls, arches, and fragments. He applied romantically influenced interpretations to sculptural symbolism. He was the first methodical medieval archaeologist in Sweden, representative of a discipline which was later to gain recognition at the university.

His further research produced a history of medieval art in Scania and a huge three-part history of Gotland art. At this time, when the history of art as such did not fall within the compass of any professorship at the university — it would not do so until 1858 — Brunius single-handedly created a niche for this discipline.

New aims of linguistic research and language teaching

Classical philology had developed in the early nineteenth century in Germany and also in Denmark in a historical and comparative direction. The new trends reached Lund rather late. In Latin, Lund had long been a preserve of the older type of teaching which laid the emphasis on the ability to speak and write correctly. Towards the middle of the century a new attitude had made its breakthrough.

In 1856 there was something of a sensation when the professor of Latin, Johan Gustaf Ek, published a programme for the graduation ceremony in Swedish instead of the customary Latin. The very title of the programme gave a hint about the new direction of philology: 'Comparative Linguistics and Latin Etymology'.

Ek's successor was Albert Lysander, the most outstanding wit in the university. Because of the position of Latin in the examination system of the day, the chair of Latin was the most onerous position in the university. In Lysander's time there arose a new form of teaching: the seminar. The objection to the traditional lectures was that they allowed students to remain mere dictation writers. The seminar system had been developed in Germany in the eighteenth century. One of the teachers of the classics in Lund on a study trip was favourably impressed by the seminar form. Together with Lysander he proposed a 'philological seminar' in Lund, directly modelled on that in Göttingen. The participants were to practise textual criticism twice a week; every other week one of them would present a paper for public discussion.

Funds were granted to allow the first seminar to begin its work in 1866. This was an important date in the academic history of Lund, and indeed of Scandinavia; it was the first instance of a teaching form which has shown its worth now for more than a hundred years. After a few decades the seminar was introduced to subject after subject in the faculties of philosophy, theology, and law.

Lysander was a versatile scholar, producing work in the field of literary history, where he introduced comparative and psychological approaches. He also wrote an introduction to the Danish philosopher Søren Kierkegaard, the first study in Swedish of any length.

His colleague Christian Cavallin worked entirely within the field of classical languages; he was best known to posterity for his Latin dictionaries, which have been used by many generations.

The first occupant of a reformed professorship which now included aesthetics, modern languages, and literature, was Carl August Hagberg. During a cultural tour of Europe he had met a number of the leading literary and philosophical figures of the day in the fashionable salons. 'Germany lives in the past, France in the future,' he wrote in his diary, entranced by the ideas of progress of the 1830s. In letters home he tells of attending lectures at the Sorbonne, of visits to Lamartine and Victor Hugo. He brought a breath of French air into the German traditions which dominated Lund. Yet it was as a communicator of English culture that he made his most important contribution. As professor in Lund from 1840 he lectured both on aesthetics, after Solger's philosophical system, and on English and French literature, analysing texts in both languages.

His unique contribution to Swedish cultural history was his translation of Shakespeare's complete plays. The twelve volumes of Hagberg's translations, which appeared between 1847 and 1851, have been reissued and performed to the present day. They remain the most impressive achievement in the art of translation into Swedish.

In the same year as his translations were completed he was elected to the Swedish Academy, which charged him with the work of beginning the great dictionary of the Swedish language which the Academy had resolved to publish. The work on the dictionary was continued by Theodor Wisén, the real founder of the scholarly tradition of Nordic philology in Lund.

Wisén's programme for the study of the Scandinavian languages was formulated in the draft of a syllabus in 1873. 'Since scientific knowledge of the mother tongue and the other modern Scandinavian languages is not possible without an understanding of their historical development, the subject must be predominantly, although not exclusively, devoted to the study of the old languages of Scandinavia.' This historical bias, with the obligatory study of Icelandic and Old Swedish, was written into the first syllabus, and it actually survived until the great reform period in the middle of the present century.

Wisén's successor as professor was Knut Söderwall. His main achievement was his dictionary of medieval Swedish, *Ordbok över svenska medeltidsspråket*, which is still an indispensable aid for readers of our medieval writings. The dictionary was the fruit of incalculable single-handed toil; it fills over 2,100 densely printed quarto pages, each with two columns.

Söderwall assumed editorship of the Swedish Academy's dictionary, *Svenska Akademiens Ordbok* — popularly abbreviated to *SAOB* — the huge and continuing result of a teamwork which has been carried on for more than a hundred years. It will have reached the last letter of the alphabet by the beginning of the next century. The accuracy in principles, method, and execution which characterizes the work was established primarily by Söderwall.

Another place of honour among Lund's nineteenth-century lexicographers is held by Dean J.E. Rietz. He had met and been inspired by the grand master of Germanic philology, Jacob Grimm. As a rural clergyman in Scania he carried on his work on his *magnum opus*, a dictionary of Swedish dialects, *Svenskt dialektlexikon*, which has recently been reissued in facsimile.

Oriental languages flourished at the university after the middle of the nineteenth century. From Uppsala came the orientalist Carl Johan Tornberg, who revived the study of the subject. He had undertaken a long study tour of Europe to learn Arabic, Persian, and Turkish from the leading orientalists in France: Silvestre de Sacy, Étienne Quatremère, and Pierre Jaubert.

His years in Lund saw the appearance of his major work as an Arabist, an edition in fourteen volumes of Ibn al-Athīr's universal history, published in Leiden between 1851 and 1876. As vice-rector of the university he wrote a programme for the study of oriental languages as a university subject in 1863. In it he presented his view of how the subject should be organized in Sweden in the future.

Philosophical schools

The period towards the middle of the nineteenth century was dominated by Hegelian philosophy in Europe, in Scandinavia, and in Lund. Hegelianism was succeeded in Sweden by the specifically Swedish form of absolute idealism which is called after the Uppsala philosopher Christopher Boström. The occupants of the two chairs of philosophy in Lund were recruited from Uppsala in the latter half of the century. The foremost spokesman of Boströmianism was Axel Nyblaeus, assistant lecturer in theoretical and practical philosophy from 1853, professor in the same subject after three years.

Boström's doctrine, which was taught for decades to come at both the Swedish universities, claims that the world around us, with its time, space, movement, and change, is merely an illusory world. The fundamental opposition in his system is between illusion and being, between sensuality and reason, in both his theoretical and his practical philosophy. God is perceived as a personal being, who encompasses in his person other persons; the world is a system of personalities.

Nyblaeus had a historical sense, and so counterbalanced the excessive abstractions of Boström's idealistic system. He was also oriented in contemporary philosophical currents, such as Theodore Parker's Christian liberalism and John Stuart Mill's social philosophy. His greatest scholarly work was *Den filosofiska forskningen i Sverige* ('Philosophical Research in Sweden'), published at the end of the nineteenth century. This two-thousand-page work is one of the most comprehensive contributions to the history of Swedish philosophy. Against the background of the development of European thought he describes personality philosophy as the line of thought characteristic of Sweden, primarily Uppsala, starting with Thorild in the eighteenth century.

There were fierce battles between Boström on the one hand and supporters of Hegel's philosophy on the other. The leading Swedish Hegelian was Johan Jacob Borelius, from 1866 professor of theoretical philosophy in Lund. He was to have a decisive influence on the philosophical life of the university until the turn of the century. In his lectures he dealt with topics from the history of philosophy, as well as psychology. He followed the development of philosophy from Nicholas of Cusa to Leibniz, Kant, and Hegel, but in the 1890s he could also devote a whole term to Spencer. In psychology he announced in 1897 — one of the years when Strindberg was in Lund — the study of topics such as dreams, psychic abnormality, and the unconscious. From the 1880s he included in the set books for the course a work on empirical psychology by his Danish colleague Harald Høffding, a book which remained on the syllabus in Lund until the 1930s.

While in Uppsala at this time philosophers and natural scientists were going their separate ways, in Lund they had a noticeable community of interests. At Borelius's private colloquies both Spencer and Darwin were discussed. Borelius himself was not at all opposed to the idea of evolution, which is of course built into the Hegelian dialectical system; yet he did object to the claim that the new evolutionism could explain existence solely from mechanical causes. For him, as for his master Hegel, physical forces were subordinate to higher spiritual principles working to accomplish a purpose.

He followed with vigilant interest the changes in the European philosophical climate, expressing his views on the left-wing Hegelian David Friedrich Strauss, the materialistic philosopher Haeckel, and the neo-Kantian Friedrich Albert Lange. He had a particular interest in Eduard von Hartmann, 'the philosopher of the unconscious'. He had met him in person and he corresponded with him, a philosophical dialogue which is extant.

His pure white hair, his luxuriant side-whiskers, his modesty, his breadth of vision, his scholarly absent-mindedness, the work on metaphysics which he never finished, all this made Borelius something of a legend in the town. The myth attracted some of the classic 'absent-minded professor' anecdotes. The most famous of these has been related countless times; it tells of how Borelius was to add his signature to a document which had been signed by the various members of the faculty. There was a large ink stain just over the place where Borelius was to put his name. The janitor who had brought the document told Borelius that the professor who had signed his name there had accidentally picked up the inkhorn instead of the sand-castor to dry the ink. Borelius laughed heartily at the distraction of his colleague Lysander. But when he handed over the piece of paper, he had signed his name Johan Jakob Inkhorn.

History — idealism and empiricism

From the middle of the nineteenth century and throughout the latter half, the new men and the new ideas in history came from Boström's and Geijer's Uppsala with its philosophical idealism. Although Wilhelm Erik Svedelius and Claes Theodor Odhner, who were in turn professors of history in Lund, stressed both the empirical character of historical science and the importance of documenting and criticizing the sources, they sought to uncover behind the empirical course of history the ideal forces — the nation, religion, humanity — which were regarded as the ultimate driving forces of history. The individual person too was considered ultimately as an instrument of higher powers. Odhner's historical textbooks for primary and secondary schools set their stamp on the teaching of history in Swedish schools for half a century. It was not until the 1880s that the pendulum began to swing in the opposite direction, from a fundamental idealism to a critical realism.

When Odhner left Lund to become director general of the National Archives, his place was taken by Martin Weibull. As a young assistant lecturer he was assigned the task of writing a history of Lund University for the bicentennial celebrations in 1868; his co-author was Elof Tegnér, a grandson of the poet and like him employed at the university library, where he later became head librarian. The work gave Weibull a sense of belonging to and a thorough familiarity with the Lund milieu.

Scandinavianism, in its Dano-Swedish form, was an important aspect of Weibull's research. In Scania and in Lund he saw the historical link between the two countries. His doctor's dissertation on eighteenth-century Scania marks his interest in provincial and local history. He published and edited collections of original documents and essays on Scanian history. With these and other works he laid the foundation of a particularly Lundensian research tradition, directed towards the early development of the former Danish provinces, and in close association with Danish historical scholarship.

The other main line of Weibull's historical research is represented by the works in which he treats the history of Sweden, Scandinavia, and France in the seventeenth century. From the middle of the 1880s we can observe Weibull's growing concern with the problems of source criticism. An essay from 1882 on the reports of the French diplomat Chanut was a contemporary breakthrough in source criticism.

His methodological orientation was international, with a certain French and Danish accent. He had little time for the subtleties of the philosophy of history. He once quoted with approval Michelet's saying: 'L'histoire, c'est la résurrection.' For Weibull himself history meant especially the resurrection of the great figures of the past; his assessment of personages like Gustav II Adolf (Gustavus Adolphus) and Christina betrays a noticeable degree of genius worship. History was still an ideologically productive discipline, central to the university ideal of the times.

Two disciplines broke away from history in the last decades of the nineteenth century: political science and geography.

The motivation for political science as a separate subject in the Oscarian era (Sweden's Victorian age) was that the university was the educational centre of the state bureaucracy. Pontus Fahlbeck, who held an extraordinary chair in history and political science from 1889, was a professional politician, a member of the Upper House. Fahlbeck emphasized the link between the social sciences and practical politics. He approached the field of sociology in a work on estates and classes, in which he described how the Swedish society of the estates was transformed into a class society. He defined his subject as 'politics and statistics', with politics understood as constitutional studies. His ambition was to reform the entire discipline according to the requirements of the day; it was thanks to him that the scope of the professorship was redefined in 1902 as political science and statistics.

The year 1897 saw the coming of a new extraordinary professorship of geography and history. Geography was still regarded as a historical subject, as was still in part political science. It was not until the next century that geography came to be ranked with the natural sciences.

The aesthetic disciplines

Cultural idealism with or without Christian overtones, liberal faith in the future, imperceptibly shading into confidence in the status quo, and Scandinavianism; these are common features of some Lund scholars within the humanities in the late nineteenth century. One of the leading figures in the group was Gustaf Ljunggren, the first professor of aesthetics and the history of art and literature. He was to play a central role at the university for many decades, with a large number of representational duties, among them the position of rector on several occasions.

After taking his doctor's degree he embarked on a lengthy educational tour; a travel scholarship took him to universities and art museums in Germany and France. His first stop was Berlin, after which he went to Tübingen to hear and meet the leading authority in the field of aesthetics, the Hegelian scholar Friedrich Theodor Vischer. The journey ended in Paris, where he attended Balzac's funeral.

On his return to Lund he was appointed in 1859 to the newly established chair of aesthetics and the history of art and literature. His earliest published works of importance were in aesthetics. After investigating various aesthetic concepts, Ljunggren turned to the more concrete sphere of literature. Through his lectures and the publications based on them, and above all through the five parts of his *Svenska vitterhetens hävder* ('The Traditions of Swedish Literature'), he laid the foundations of research into the history of literature in Sweden. His chief model was Hermann Hettner, the German historian of art and literature, who had published in the 1840s an attack on speculative aesthetics, and who built his own account of the European literature of the Enlightenment on the solid foundation of history and documentation. Ljunggren organized his major work on the Swedish Enlightenment and Romanticism in the same way. Within the sphere of art history he lectured and wrote on Winckelmann and Ehrensvärd; he also produced a massive volume on the stately homes of Scania.

The liberal with the ardent ideas of freedom gradually mellowed into an old man of rather conservative taste and ideology. In the Swedish Academy he succeeded another Lundensian littérateur, the liberal Johan Henrik Thomander. He followed the literary developments in contemporary Scandinavia with an attentive and critical eye. Extant lecture notes show that in 1872 he had already considered Georg Brandes's view that 'a poet should always raise questions for debate'. This was a speedy reply to Brandes's introductory lecture the previous year, the first in a series on the main currents of European culture.

Ljunggren's home became a centre for the academic social life of the upper bourgeoisie. It was visited by guests like Hans Christian Andersen and other Danish poets, by professors from Copenhagen, and by the English Scandinavianist Edmund Gosse.

When Ljunggren retired from his chair in 1891, his successor was Henrik Schück from Uppsala. As so often, the change of person also meant a change of scholarly climate. Schück represented the academic ideal of a later generation. He had little time for post-Hegelian aesthetics. He was — or tried to be — a pure empiricist. His ideal of scholarship was close to positivism. He made his first study trip not to Germany but to England. This was in connection with his interest in Renaissance drama and Shakespeare. His years in Lund saw the appearance of *Illustrerad svensk litteraturhistoria* ('Illustrated History of Swedish Literature'), written in collaboration Karl Warburg. Schück's contributions covered the period from the earliest Old Swedish literature down to Sweden's days as a great power.

In his lectures and seminars Schück treated widely differing areas: English literature, foreign influence on medieval Swedish literature, epochs in the history of art, among them the Italian Renaissance; it was he who made a set course book of Burckhardt's *Geschichte der Renaissance in Italien.*

After a few years Schück left Lund — with no regrets — to return to Uppsala, where he continued his mammoth work as a historian of literature. He attained such a position that his name and his work became practically synonymous with the history of Swedish literature.

The natural sciences — a change of paradigm

In Lund the breakaway from the romantic research traditions of idealistic speculation in the second half of the nineteenth century came earliest and most forcefully in the natural sciences. The scientific foundation for positivism was laid by men like Auguste Comte and John Stuart Mill.

Science and medicine advanced with the aid of strictly empirical and experimental methods; these subjects led the way for other disciplines. The change was discernible first in botany and zoology, where Darwin's theory of evolution changed perspectives radically. The change of scientific paradigm found a concrete illustration in the appointment in 1879 of Fredrik Wilhelm Areschough to the chair which had previously been occupied by Jacob Georg Agardh. Agardh had followed in his distinguished father's footsteps, doing his most important work in the field of algae, where he won international recognition. He had described a large number of new species and ordered them in groups, systematically and morphologically. But his view of nature was, like his father's, idealistic, almost Platonic. 'Every organism must be regarded as formed according to a certain type, a certain plan, must represent as it were an idea.' Such was his formulation of his fundamental outlook in his *Växtsystemets metodologi* ('The Methodology of the Plant System'). He considered the species to be essentially constant — a parallel to the way contemporary philosophical historians viewed the nation or religion as ideal entities in the same way.

When Charles Darwin published his book *On the Origin of Species* in 1859, he sent copies to contemporary European scientists who could be expected to be interested in his theories. In this way a volume with Darwin's dedication ended up on Agardh's desk; it is still preserved in 'Agardhianum', the Department of Botany. Agardh rejected Darwin's ideas completely.

His successor Areschough was one of the few Swedish natural scientists to be fascinated by Darwin's theory of evolution as soon as it appeared. As a systematician he did research in the genus *Rubus*. 'I have chosen this genus chiefly to test the Darwinian theory, with which I agree more and more,' he wrote in a letter in 1879. The resistance to evolutionary ideas was still so strong that it was considered almost scandalous that Areschough, when appointed professor in 1879, held his inaugural lecture on Darwinism, delivering devastating criticism of the objections to the theory of evolution. He developed the theory further by showing that abrupt changes in species formation within the genus *Rubus* could take place 'by leaps'; in this way he anticipated de Vries's teachings on mutations.

Another branch of science which Areschough introduced to Sweden was plant anatomy, which he had studied under the most distinguished plant anatomist of the day, Hugo von Mohl in Tübingen; in the 1870s Areschough added a course in plant anatomy to his syllabus.

The opposition to the theory of evolution as Darwin further refined it in *The Descent of Man* was due to the fact that it ran counter to the Christian belief in creation and Man's unique, God-given position in it. Areschough's colleague

ON

THE ORIGIN OF SPECIES

BY MEANS OF NATURAL SELECTION,

OR THE

PRESERVATION OF FAVOURED RACES IN THE STRUGGLE
FOR LIFE.

By CHARLES DARWIN, M.A.,

FELLOW OF THE ROYAL, GEOLOGICAL, LINNÆAN, ETC., SOCIETIES;
AUTHOR OF 'JOURNAL OF RESEARCHES DURING H. M. S. BEAGLE'S VOYAGE
ROUND THE WORLD.'

LONDON:
JOHN MURRAY, ALBEMARLE STREET.
1859.

as professor of zoology, August Quennerstedt, has become better known to posterity for his stubborn resistance to Darwinism than for his research expeditions as a young man to Arctic regions or his studies of infusorian fauna in Sweden. From the 1860s and some thirty years on he waged a violent polemic against Darwin's ideas in lectures and articles, some of which appeared, typically enough, in a Christian educational periodical.

Despite such resistance, however, Darwin's revolutionary theory penetrated the zoologists' citadel in Lund. Comparative anatomy was one branch of science where observations would confirm Darwin's view of evolution. Actually, Quennerstedt's predecessor as professor of zoology, Fredrik Wahlgren, had introduced the study of comparative anatomy to his subject. During his studies in Germany and Holland, Wahlgren had learnt the techniques of microscopic examination; by greatly enlarging the objects it was possible to obtain a clearer view of the structure and function of their organs.

Two young Lund zoologists, Wilhelm Leche and David Bergendal, both studied at Heidelberg under the German anatomist Carl Gegenbaur, founder of modern morphology. Gegenbaur was one of the scholars whose work on comparative anatomy and observations of the mutual relations of animal species lent empirical support to Darwin's theory of descent. Both these young scholars returned to Lund as enthusiastic advocates of evolution; Leche became professor of zoology at Stockholm, while Bergendal succeeded Quennerstedt in Lund. Bergendal's work marked the beginning of a new epoch for the department of zoology. In his research he used the microscope technique he had learnt in Germany; he gave courses in comparative anatomy, embryology, and histology.

Darwinism and the theory of evolution influenced developments far outside the field of science. It gave a generation of young intellectuals an almost religious faith in evolution in the social field as well. It also contributed to new perceptions of nature and new lyrical sentiments in the young poets of the day, among them Ola Hansson from Lund.

In two other scientific subjects, physics and astronomy, there were equally thoroughgoing changes in perspective at roughly the same time. Physics in Europe had taken giant strides forward during the nineteenth century; from having been applied mathematics the previous century, it grew to become an empirical science with a new theoretical foundation. Lundensian physics had its first classical period in a department building newly erected in the 1880s. Today a memorial plaque there reminds us of an important contribution to the subject: 'Johannes Robert Rydberg here laid the foundation for our knowledge of the structure of atoms.'

Rydberg's research was significant for two areas in particular: for the shaping of modern atomic theory and for spectral analysis. Rydberg gave the ordinal numbers of the elements in the periodic system the new name of atomic numbers, thus assigning a greater significance to them. By means of spectral analysis he studied the emission spectra of the elements, demonstrating that the wavelength of the spectral line emitted by an atom can be stated in a formula with a few constants; one of these is common to all elements and is known to scientists the world over as the Rydberg constant.

Many contemporaries had difficulty in envisaging how momentous for the future Rydberg's research was to prove. However, the young Niels Bohr in Copenhagen, one of the founders of modern atomic physics, read Rydberg's writings at an early stage, quoted him in his first dissertations, and was inspired by him to develop the research further. Moreover, when a map was made of the lunar terrain after the first American landing on the moon, one of the mountains was given the fitting name of Rydberg after the Lund physicist.

In astronomy too, Lund attained a high rank from the end of the nineteenth century. The arrival of Carl Vilhelm Charlier as director of the department of astronomy in 1897 marked the start of a lively period in its history. He came from Uppsala, from a background which mixed atheism and political radicalism with a fundamentally scientific outlook. The process by which he was appointed was complex and full of intrigue: he was regarded with disfavour by the powers that were in Lund University, but his academic qualifications, including work at the Pulkova Observatory in Russia and at the modern observatory in Berlin, were particularly high.

His earliest research and lectures were devoted to celestial mechanics and the theory of the movements of heavenly bodies. He then went on to study the structure of the Milky Way. He set as his goal the development of exact mathematical methods for analysing as accurately as possible the huge volume of observational material which was beginning to flow in from the giant observatories in America.

As a member of the governing body of the Astronomische Gesellschaft in Germany he presided over the international astronomical congress in Lund in 1904, which ended on Tycho Brahe's island of Hven. In the 1920s he was invited to lecture at Berkeley; the topic was stellar statistics. He published a number of studies in this subject, as well as in mathematical statistics. In 1907 he lectured in Lund on probability calculations. It was on his initiative that mathematical statistics became an independent subject at Lund University. One of his pupils who had taken his doctorate in astronomy went over to mathematical statistics and became the first professor of the subject: Sven Dag Wicksell.

New directions in medicine

Generations of scholars in France, Austria, and Germany had helped to develop medicine in pace with the natural sciences. It was mostly via Austria and Germany that new impulses in medical science came to Lund. Almost all the students at the Lund faculty at this time undertook long study trips abroad.

In the middle of the century Rudolf Virchow in Berlin had elaborated the study of cells and propounded the thesis that pathological changes in the body are due to cellular disorders. In Vienna the pathologist Karl von Rokitanski had established pathological anatomy as the basis of medical knowledge and treatment. The young Gustaf Sven Trägårdh from Lund had studied with both these authorities. On his return to his own university town he began in the 1860s a series of lectures on pathological anatomy, and he later became profesor of practical medicine. Trägårdh was one of the founders of the Lund Medical Society, formed in 1862 with a view to giving members the opportunity to follow current developments in various areas through lectures and discussions.

Another Lundensian medical scholar who had studied abroad was Victor Odenius. For four months in Berlin he had attended Virchow's lectures and autopsies in Berlin. He had also visited a number of foreign universities, Vienna, Bonn, Würzburg, Paris, Brussels, and Leiden, everywhere coming into contact with the pioneers of the latest medical research. In 1875 he held his inaugural lecture on the new theories of the causes of infectious diseases. As professor of theoretical medicine and forensic medicine (as the subject was now called), he strove to give a central place to the study of pathology. It was during his time that the first department of pathology was built in Lund.

At the end of the nineteenth century the medical faculty had ten professors and five lecturers. Two of the foremost members had been students in Uppsala but now became loyal Lundensians: Seved Ribbing and Jacques Borelius. During their time and thanks to their combined efforts a new arrangement for clinical teaching was introduced, according to which the senior physicians in the five departments of the hospital were to be professors in the corresponding subjects in the faculty of medicine. This meant a close association of research and teaching.

When Seved Ribbing became professor of practical medicine in 1888, his inaugural lecture dealt with the foundations and founders of modern therapy. On the private side he was in great demand as a doctor for rich and poor alike. He was often to be seen driving his carriage to visit patients. Alongside his work as a practising doctor he was often called on to deliver lectures to the general public. He also wrote a series of popularizing medical brochures.

Ribbing's colleague, Jacques Borelius, had written his doctor's dissertation about a topic of current interest at the time: the development and application of antisepsis. He became lecturer in surgery in 1890 and professor of the same subject nine years later. He introduced a new epoch in surgery, which had long been neglected. His first action was the modernization of the surgical clinic. As a surgeon he became one of the foremost of his generation. He was also a unifying force at the Nordic surgeons' congresses. A study trip in the 1910s brought him into contact with the leading surgeons of the day in the United

States: Cushing, Murphy, and the Mayo brothers. But his main achievements were in his practical work as professor of surgery and as an organizer, in his capacity of hospital director.

Two modern linguists

The positivism which had made its breakthrough in science and medicine also became important in the humanities, where linguistics was the first subject to be influenced by the new scholarly ideal. The evolutionary theories which had been confirmed by the natural scientists were adopted by comparative philologists who sought laws for the regular evolution of language. In Germany the main advocate of the comparative method was Max Müller; in Denmark the leading name in the now flourishing study of Sanskrit and Iranian was N.L. Westergaard, alongside his Copenhagen colleague Vilhelm Thomsen, whose subject was comparative linguistics.

All these scholars influenced Esaias Tegnér the Younger; he had close personal contacts with the two Danes. The first series of lectures which Tegnér held in Lund in 1877, in the year when he became professor of oriental languages, was entirely in the spirit of the modern comparative philology. He lectured on Proto-Indo-European and the regular sound changes by which it developed into the separate language families. His attempt to solve the problem of the Indo-Iranian palatals has earned him a footnote in the early history of Indo-European philology.

While his lectures covered Proto-Indo-European and the other languages which fell within the scope of his professorship, Iranian and Arabic, his written work was mostly devoted to modern Swedish. His work of 1880, *Språkets makt över tanken* ('The Power of Language over Thought'), was already famous for its title, which had originally been the title of his inaugural lecture. In the introduction to the book he outlines a programme for the empirical, positivistic study of language after the model of the Germans. He declared that 'the method of linguistics is now entirely the same as that of the natural sciences,' and he rejected the speculative linguists' view of language as a living 'organism'. He took language to be a 'system' which had arisen through convention, and he saw the essential function of words as 'tools for communication'. To this communicative function of language he added its role in creating national identity.

In the twentieth century most of his energy was expended on two projects: one was the Swedish Academy's dictionary, of which he was in charge for a time, while the other was the new translation of the Bible, completed in 1917. His work on the Old Testament brought him back to the field of oriental languages.

By virtue of his name, background, and origin, Esaias Tegnér the Younger was firmly anchored in Lund. As an old man — he lived to the age of eighty-five — with ample white curls and a quietly harmonious personality, he became the town's *genius loci*.

The modern European languages had been rather neglected in a university where Latin had dominated for so long. The swing in favour of the modern languages took place in the last decades of the nineteenth century. The chair of 'modern European linguistics and modern literature', as the subject was called, was filled in 1878 by Volter Edvard Lidforss. His lectures covered the entire broad field of his professorship. He also translated *Don Quixote* and Dante's *Divina Commedia*, providing a learned commentary on the latter.

In a letter of 1879 Lidforss characterized the subject which he represented as 'completely apocryphal' and expressed with good reason the opinion that it should be split as soon as possible and replaced by two chairs, of Germanic and Romance languages, respectively. This division did in fact take place, but not until 1888, when the Romance languages acquired an extraordinary professorship; Lidforss himself retained responsibility for teaching and examination in the Germanic languages.

Lidforss maintained contact with contemporary linguistic science through foreign travel and attending congresses. In a letter he praises himself for being the first to have introduced and lectured on the subject of phonetics. Lidforss was also active in the establishment of a philological seminary for the teaching of modern languages. In a statement of 1885 he stressed the urgency of employing native speakers to teach the three major European languages — the university had previously made do with a single language master. Uppsala had already appointed foreign lectors, and a parliamentary resolution granted the same to Lund in 1889. In the present century foreign language teaching has been successively expanded, with foreign lectors in, among other languages, Italian, Spanish, Romanian, Modern Greek, Finnish, and a number of Slavic and oriental languages.

The university jubilee

In May 1868 the university celebrated its bicentennial with all the attendant pomp. At ten o'clock the procession set off for the cathedral. Outside the university building in Lundagård stood the academic guard, two ranks of men still armed with halberds. The university rector wore the gold-edged cape of purple velvet and the wide-brimmed hat of his office.

The students in the procession wore their white caps, the emblem which had been adopted the previous year by the students' union. The union had been formed as an independent corporation in 1867; the official adoption of the white cap was in fact one of the first resolutions passed by the new union.

When the procession of men in tails and white caps reached the cathedral, King Karl XV took up his place to listen to speeches in Latin and Swedish and a choral cantata. After this the representatives of the foreign universities came forward, from Germany the rector of Rostock University, from Denmark the philologists Madvig and Westergaard, from Finland the poet Topelius.

On the second and third days, degrees were conferred on members of the four faculties. Crown Prince Oscar was appointed to play a major role, that of lighting the magnificent fireworks on one of the evenings of the celebrations. He was also solemnly crowned with a laurel wreath during an improvised ceremony in the cathedral on the last day of the conferring of degrees. This was the first time such homage had been paid to a royal personage by a Swedish university. The festivities were a symbolic reflection of the position of the university, subject to the highest temporal and spiritual powers in the country.

It was a provincial university of modest size which commemorated the two hundred years of its existence. The decidedly Southern Swedish character is seen in the figures showing the recruitment of students and teachers. In the jubilee year of 1868, of the 338 students no less than 212 belonged to the Scanian nations. An overwhelming majority of the university dons were also of Scanian or Southern Swedish origin.

A decade later the University of Copenhagen celebrated its fourth centennial; the year was 1879. Lund was represented by a large delegation. The Danish and Swedish scholars who met on that occasion made an agreement to commence regular university meetings. For generations of academics on both sides of the sound this was an impetus to contacts on both personal and scholarly levels. The meetings took on a deeper significance in both world wars, as manifestations of a shared intellectual front. At one of the university meetings in the inter-war years the Danish literary historian Vilhelm Andersen evoked a long time perspective to pay tribute to the sister university: 'Lund University, which was founded in former Danish lands, has in the course of time acted as a channel for the introduction of the Danish spirit into Sweden.'

'Danish spirit' included the medium of the Danish language. As a result of the practical Scandinavianism of the twentieth century, the subject of the Scandinavian languages was expanded from the 1920s to include courses in

Danish held by Danish lectors. The Nordic lectorships in the department were given official status the following decade.

The new university building and the new library

At the time of its bicentennial Lund University with its 338 students was about the same size as the small-town German universities of Rostock and Münster. At the same time Uppsala had 1,216 students, Bonn and Halle slightly more; Berlin University had between four and five thousand. It took nearly a hundred years for Lund to reach the same figure.

In the latter half of the nineteenth century Lund University had grown too large not only for its old organizational forms but also, in a purely concrete sense, for its old premises. After the 1840s a number of new departmental buildings were erected; they bear witness to the expansion in science and medicine.

The building phase of the nineteenth century culminated in 1882 with the completion of a new university building, a creation of the architect Helgo Zettervall. It stands as a definitive monument to nineteenth-century humanism, as can be read in the symbolic language of the architecture. It is an advanced example of representational architecture in imitation classical style. Its creator had visited Rome, but must also have been influenced by Karl Friedrich Schinkel's classical designs for the Altes Museum and the Schauspielhaus in Berlin.

The university building, with its variously interpretable symbols of art and wisdom — Medusa heads, owls, lyres — was inaugurated in 1882. The dedication ceremony was attended by representatives of the other Scandinavian universities, the Archbishop of Uppsala and the Bishop of Lund in full pontificals, representatives of parliament and the government led by King Oscar II; he presented as a gift the gilded rector's chain which is still in use today. The ceremony was yet another mark of the symbolic place of the university in the Nordic community and in the authoritarian society of the Oscarian era.

When all the festivities were over the university building could come into use in its everyday functions. On the ground floor there were rooms of appropriate dignity for the rector, the registry, and the administration; the four faculties and the Consistory were allotted rooms for meetings and examinations. In the basement the overcrowded Historical Museum had room for a time to

Runic stone in the University Library. The oldest Norse 'manuscript' in the library, the stone was found near the place where the library is situated.

display its archaeological collections. On the first floor there were lecture theatres; the top floor had a portrait gallery and a coin showcase. The functions of the building have changed through time; with the triumph of the bureaucrats in the 1960s and 1970s most of the rooms have been claimed for the swelling administration.

After the new university building had been dedicated, the university library was able to take over all the floors of the old Lundagård building, where it had had limited space since the seventeenth century. The old ceremonial hall — the Caroline Hall — was turned into a book storeroom and a new reading room was appointed. Yet it was all a temporary arrangement. In the course of the nineteenth century the book collections had grown considerably. By 1900 there were around 200,000 volumes, of which 5,000 were manuscripts. Under the direction of the head librarian Elof Tegnér, who now ran the library where his grandfather had once been deputy librarian, the books were newly catalogued according to author and subject.

The amount of space in the Lundagård building proved insufficient after a few decades. Between 1902 and 1907 a new library building was erected on Helgonabacken; it was built of red brick with mouldings and ornamentation in limestone. During the twentieth century it has been extended and rebuilt in stages to accommodate the growth of the book collection, which was estimated to comprise about two and a half million volumes in 1980.

Lack of space brought about a division of the book collection in the 1970s. The humanities and theology have been allowed to remain in the building on Helgonabacken, while science and medicine have been moved to a new library building in the part of town where the science departments are housed. This split was one of many signs of the times, indicating the separation of 'the two cultures'.

There is a library for undergraduates in a separate building. The newspaper library has been housed in separate premises on the edge of town. Lund is the only Swedish library outside Stockholm to retain the right to an original copy of every Swedish daily newspaper. This is one of the material foundations for the active press research which has grown up in Lund in recent decades.

Young radicals, coteries, and carnivals

The generation of young students of the 1880s who entered the atrium of the university building with its marble floor and columns, or the ornate great hall with its character of an ancient temple, were not all prepared to accept the cultural and educational ideals which were manifest there. The opposition between the conservative desire to preserve traditions and the radical, youthful need to rebel is a constantly recurring theme in every university town. Now, however, the opposition of old and new was more evident than at any previous time.

A feature common to all the contemporary writers with an academic background was that they all sought to come to terms with the university milieu. The same critical view of antiquated learning and the empty phrases of idealism which August Strindberg expressed in his descriptions of student life in Uppsala is also found in a generation of young authors from Lund, who mark a break with tradition on every important front.

Literary accounts of student days in Lund suggest that there was little time for study. For the majority of students, however, reality was rather different. The phalanx of young, rebellious students of the 1880s produced some of the foremost teachers and researchers Lund has ever seen, with new values, a new impetus, and a view of scholarship born of a new era. Here, as so often in the history of science and learning, the break with tradition is the very heartbeat marking the rhythmic alternation of innovation and consolidation: renewal occurs when a new generation takes the stage.

The young intelligentsia dominated a radical student club which called itself D.U.G. (an abbreviation of *De unga gubbarne* 'the young fogeys'). They all had a foundation in modern empirical science, having read Darwin, Mill, and Spencer. They all shared a vigorous faith in evolution combined with left-wing political sympathies. Many were to make notable contributions to science and medicine: the botanist Bengt Lidforss, first lecturer and then professor; Elis Strömgren, who became lecturer in astronomy at Kiel, later professor in the same subject at Copenhagen and director of the astronomical observatory there; Paul Rosenius, physician and naturalist, who has left us the classic picture of the D.U.G. group in his documentary novel *De unga gubbarne*.

In the 1880s the members of the group upheld their views in discussion evenings at the Academic Union and at meetings of the students' union. It was D.U.G. who got the students' union in 1889 to organize a commemoration of the centenary of the French revolution. It was also D.U.G. who brought about the cancellation in the autumn of the same year of the traditional torchlight parade in memory of Karl XII.

The Great Debating Society attracted attention with its debates about Christianity, in which older academics also took part. The ensuing discussions were to continue for decades, with Lidforss and other advocates of the theory of evolution crossing swords with defenders of the Christian view of life.

The D.U.G. group was formally disbanded in 1891, but the leading figures continued to make themselves heard in other contexts. The next generation of students revived the society, now under the name of D.Y.G. (*De yngre gubbarne* 'the younger fogeys').

The 1890s brought new currents into student life in Lund. The great hall of the Academic Union was still the arena for public discussion evenings, but a smaller, more intimate place provided a home and a name for a coterie of aesthetes and Bohemians who were to leave their mark on the literary milieu of the student town. This was Café Tua. The name came from the Italian singer

Teresina Tua, who had visited Lund several times in the 1880s and captivated her young audiences. The Tua circle read modern literature, French symbolism and German *fin de siècle* poetry. Nietzsche's philosophy of the superman was grafted on to Darwin's theory of natural selection.

The socialist movement in Sweden had already gained a foothold in the D.U.G. group. A new association in closer contact with social reality was the Students' and Workers' Society, formed in 1893. The inspiration for this association was the Fabian Society of London, which disseminated ideas of a socialist nature through publications and lectures.

Lund at the end of the nineteenth century was characterized equally by debates on the philosophy of life, by diligent study, and by boisterous student life. The spring festivities in May caused student joy to burst into flower. From the 1850s, spring celebrations had been stage-managed according to a deliberate plan, with a printed programme. A masked procession which the student nations of Scania organized on the first of May, 1859, is usually reckoned as the first Lund carnival. Later on the spring carnival became the concern of the entire students' union. The carnival processions were often planned around a contemporary theme — the unification of Italy, the introduction of representation for the four estates, current political events in America or Greece, Andrée's expedition by balloon to the North Pole.

The Lundensian carnival and its programme received its characteristic style in the days when Axel Wallengren, one of the Tua coterie, sat on the carnival committee. In 1888 the title of the carnival was 'The Tragedy of the World'. Wallengren (who called himself 'Falstaff, fakir') penned the following picture of the masquerade procession in a poem which begins:

> The shifting forms of 'The World's Tragedy'
> Proceed in motley order through the town,
> Where they have gathered one spring day, to drown
> The sorrows of this life in laughter's Lethe.

In the printed carnival programmes and carnival newspapers, with their hilarious torrent of absurdities, Axel Wallengren polished the Mark Twain-inspired style which was to make him famous in his books *Envar sin egen professor* ('Every Man his Own Professor') and *Envar sin egen gentleman* ('Every Man his Own Gentleman'), of which the former was translated into German.

The exhilarant carnivals of the ancient Greeks, with the feast of Dionysus in Athens and the attendant *komos* 'revelry', gave rise to comedy, often lascivious jokes and comic parodies of contemporary philosophers and writers.

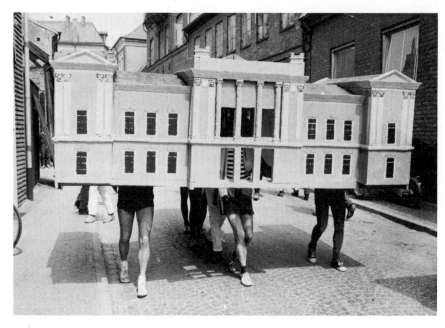

A brave attempt by Lund students to get the university on its feet. From the student carnival in 1966.

The spring festivities associated with the Lund carnival have similarly given rise to the type of burlesque student revue known as *spex* (student slang for Latin *spectaculum*). The first proper *spex* in Lund came in 1886. It was entitled 'Gerda'; the name and the theme both refer to the title of an unfinished epic by Tegnér.

It was to this place of contradictions, with the clash of gaiety and gravity, of old and new, that August Strindberg came in 1896, driven by the wind after his European odyssey. In his own words: 'Pursued by the furies, I finally found myself in December 1896 lashed down in the little university town of L. in Sweden. A conglomeration of petty bourgeois houses around a cathedral, a palatial university building and a library, constituting an oasis of civilization on the great plain of Southern Sweden.'

Strindberg sought the company of a young group of scholars and writers. In his notes *From an Occult Diary* and in his autobiographical *Legends* he has left us his — often bewildering — pictures of the milieu and society of Lund.

From the foreword which he wrote for the posthumous edition of Axel Wallengren's works, Strindberg's classic words are often quoted: 'Lund, the little secretive town which can never be fathomed; closed, impenetrable;

friendly but not with open arms; serious and industrious as a monastery, where one would never go of one's own accord, but which one nevertheless leaves with a sense of regret; which one feels like running away from, but where one always returns.'

The entry of the female students

For more than two hundred years the university had the atmosphere of an exclusive gentlemen's club. Women's faces are seldom seen in older histories of the university, which may of course be because they were written by men. Yet women have naturally had a number of important but often forgotten roles, whether in the centre or on the periphery of university life.

A professor's wife could assist her husband in numerous practical ways, but her most important role was still to ensure the reproduction of academic society. Anyone who wished to trace the genealogies of Lund University would be struck by the extent to which the same names recur, with academic offices becoming almost hereditary, the property of a restricted number of scholarly families.

A group of women often encountered in older student accounts are the landladies, often prudish clergymen's widows, and the worthy, unbribable, and indispensable cleaners. By contrast, nineteenth-century memoirs — before the breakthrough of naturalism — are almost completely silent on the topic of the prostitutes who played an important role in the vacuum of student society, where female company was otherwise absent. In the years from 1877 to 1907 the police lists state the number of prostitutes, who were legally bound to undergo medical examination, as 117. Paul Rosenius, in his book about The Young Fogeys, is brutally honest when he puts the following words in Axel Wallengren's mouth: 'This quiet little town with its huge church is an insidious seducer of youth. There are no other outlets for youthful glee than two great sewers: the filthy pubs and the old whores.'

The arrival of female students brought about a radical change in the university, which was probably the most decisive change in the history of the academic mentality. But the change occurred in stages, slowly and with delayed effect. The question of whether women should be entitled to study and sit examinations with the same rights as men was considered for the first time in Lund's faculties and Consistory in 1867. There were conflicting views in the four faculties, where the issue was discussed with arguments typical of the day, about offended modesty, the putative destiny of women, and the threat of seduction. The settlement of the question took some time, referred as it was to higher authorities; not until 1870 did women gain the right to sit a university entrance examination at the secondary schools. In 1873 the king ruled that women should have the right to benefit from public education and sit all examinations at the universities, with the exception of examinations in the theology faculty and the licentiate in law. Many decades were to elapse before these last restrictions were lifted.

In practice the going for women was hard at the beginning. The first female student was enrolled in 1880, and the rest of the decade saw the matriculation of fifteen in all; there were slightly more in the following decade. A female students' union was formed in 1900 with a view to protecting their special interests.

Despite the slow start, however, Lund was relatively far advanced by European standards. A Lund student who visited Berlin in 1896 reported in a newspaper article his surprise and indignation that women at this time still did not have the right to take examinations at Berlin University, and were not even allowed to attend lectures. In a concrete example he told how the great historian Heinrich von Treitschke broke off a lecture when he caught sight of a woman in the auditorium and politely but resolutely escorted her out of the door of this holy of holies. In comparison it may be added that Heidelberg University permitted women to read scientific subjects ten years later than Lund, in 1890, but only in 1900 did it give them the general right to study other subjects.

University extension

The university had long been a closed society in other respects as well as being an exclusively male preserve. Admittedly, the wall around Lundagård — that symbolic boundary — had been demolished, and the university's independent jurisdiction had been abolished in the middle of the century. Yet the character of a closed guild had been retained as long as possible in the intellectual milieu, although a few individual lecturers in the history of literature early in the nineteenth century had been able to attract the general public to the lecture theatres. The university was and continued to be a privileged educational centre for future officials in the public sector: clergymen, teachers, lawyers, and doctors.

Tendencies towards a rupture of this isolation appeared in the last decades of the nineteenth century. A new interest in education had grown within the labour movement. Lecture societies were formed, with their roots in the Workers' Institutes founded in the nineteenth century. Contact was sought with the universities, where there was a desire to bring the results of research to social strata other than the privileged few. Many of the younger generation of democratic academics were convinced that if learning were made accessible to everyone, it would help to bridge the gaps between the classes. In Scania the first lecture society was formed in Malmö in 1883; many Lund academics from various faculties were engaged as speakers.

The initiative also came from the universities themselves. They provided adult education through academic summer courses, the first of which was organized in Uppsala in 1893, the second in Lund the following year. Of the more than a hundred participants in Lund's first summer course, most were elementary school teachers who lacked high-school qualifications and were therefore not formally entitled to study at the university. Teaching was done through the medium of lectures and excursions.

The direction of the first summer course was entrusted to the professor of medicine, Seved Ribbing. As a young man he had belonged to Fredrika Bremer's circle and had been affected by her liberal ideas. His own orientation was distinctly Anglo-Saxon; in England the idea of university extension had already been put into practice. The university summer courses persisted in scarcely changed forms into the 1920s. They disappeared in the world of the new media, definitively after the arrival of radio. There was a sort of continuation in the 1930s and 1940s with the summer vacation courses for foreign students.

All generations did their cultural duty in popular lecturing; members of D.U.G. also served as 'peasant lecturers', as they were known. This educational enterprise was carried along on a wave of enthusiasm, but it could also bring in a significant income for those who lectured frequently; several professorial mansions were built with the aid of these lectures.

These extra-mural lectures are an undeniable sign of the dominant role which the university had adopted in public consciousness in the late nineteenth and early twentieth centuries. French sociological culture historians speak of *l'époque universitaire*, which in France lasted roughly until the 1920s. The same term can be used for Sweden. The initiative and the guidance still came from the universities themselves. This university dominance applied to the school system, where the institution of the *censor* guaranteed that the final examination for the leaving certificate maintained university standards. It applied also to the church, which took its bishops and archbishops from among the professors of the theological faculties. It applied also to the press and the young radio service, where the leading positions were filled by people with university degrees. A philosophy professor who was also a journalist and a public lecturer aptly described the trend as being less a question of democratizing culture than of cultivating democracy. It has been observed of a comparable period of university dominance that university professors can achieve a predominant role within their society only under specific conditions. 'Above all, they can become and remain a functional ruling class only during a particular phase in the material development of their country. They thrive between the primary agrarian level of economic organization and full industrialization' (Fritz Ringer, *The Decline of the German Mandarins*, 1969). Whatever relations between base and superstructure may be assumed to have existed, the conditions noted for Germany agree well with those in Sweden: a period of dominance followed by a decrease in the influence of the university on society from the end of World War I.

After the 1920s and 1930s the older type of adult education witnessed a continuous decline. This was mostly due to a changed cultural situation and new types of cultural communication. Other approaches to university extension have been tried in recent times, with university study circles and extra-mural departments. The Extra-Mural Department at Lund provides a rich and varied range of teaching, which has also been directed towards new social groups: immigrants and pensioners. Yet it is mainly radio and to some extent also television which have taken over. In the 1920s the radio service opened a new forum for academics, who appeared in literary review programmes and had the opportunity to present their work in popular form. The university's desire to extend its educational scope has also been displayed in the contributions made by Lund scholars in recent decades to encyclopaedias and reference works. One of these, *Svensk uppslagsbok*, the last (to date) to provide adequate bibliographical references, had its editorial board in Lund, based in the University Library.

Another testimonial to industrious research and the desire to make it accessible to the public is an inexhaustible reference work known as *Bevingade ord* ('Winged Words'). The editor of this dictionary of phrases and quotations was a man in the long tradition of Lundensian lexicography, Pelle Holm. He was editor-in-chief of the Swedish Academy's dictionary and also edited several revisions of the Swedish Academy's orthographical word list, on top of which he was active as a popular lecturer around the country and on the radio.

Work like this carried the late-nineteenth-century adult education movement into our own century, in changed forms, and beyond the period of university dominance.

Chapter 4
The Twentieth Century
From Autocracy via Democracy
to Bureaucracy

The University Quadrangle, an architectural whole which reflects the idea of the university as a unity and a totality.

When the cathedral watchman blew his horn at a quarter past ten on the last night of December 1899, the doors were opened to reveal the glory of new electric lighting. At the turn-of-the-century service the prime professor of theology delivered a sermon in which he described the past century as a time of progress and development, with new inventions such as X-rays and telephones — Lund had recently acquired a telephone network — but also as an age of growing unbelief. Then the organ began to play and the bells rang. Two of the tower bells had survived from the day when the university was first dedicated. The sounds of the old and the new met in the air: when the bells fell silent, the Workers' Song Club sang in chorus in Lundagård.

At the start of the new century Lund had between sixteen and seventeen thousand inhabitants. The student catalogue gave the number of students as 581. Over three hundred of these belonged to the faculty of philosophy (arts and sciences). The next in size was the faculty of law, with 117 students; then came medicine with 78; the smallest was theology with 71.

The academic staff was 105 strong (of whom nine had telephones). There were 27 ordinary professors, 13 extraordinary. The lecturers numbered 55. Each of the three main European languages had a lector. There were likewise the three exercise masters. One of them became well known beyond the boundaries of the town, and indeed the country: the conductor Alfred Berg — known as Father Berg — who led the student choir to repeated triumphs.

The all-round scholar or polymath had not yet completely disappeared, but the type of researcher which became characteristic of the new century was the specialist. Indeed, the professorial type had undergone decisive changes over the centuries. The eighteenth-century university professor was a learned collector, arranger, and systematizer. The romantic ideal of the early nineteenth century was the brilliant expounder of ancient texts and nature's mysteries. After the middle of the century the scholarly ideal was incarnated in yet another new type, the empiricist, the positivist seeking the laws which govern biological evolution or linguistic change. The twentieth-century professor, the scientific specialist, had stricter standards demanding exact observation of detail, verification, and critical evaluation of the evidence.

Within each subject the professor had practically autocratic powers. He determined — with the benevolent approval of the faculty and the chancellor — the scope and composition of the courses of study; he chose term by term the subjects for his lectures and seminars, usually connected to his own field of research. He tended to ensure that his own published works were required reading for the examinations. In this way there was created a homogeneity within the disciplines, with generation after generation of students being schooled — especially through the seminars — in the scholarly outlook and method of the professor. Research within the various disciplines was steadily growing, without directives from government authorities or civil servants.

It was evident right from the beginning that Lund derived its character from its professors. A professors' quarter grew up east of Helgonabacken, where professors built detached houses; later generations of professors live at best in terraced houses.

The examinations in the four faculties led to bachelors' degrees and licentiates; in 1907 the philosophy faculty introduced a special Master of Philosophy qualification. The scope of the examination for the bachelor's degree was reduced by cutting the number of compulsory subjects. The examination for the licentiate, which had previously required two or more subjects, was now limited to one. On the other hand, doctoral dissertations grew in size, with increased demands on mastery of reference literature and source documentation. From the modest booklets which had been accepted as doctors' theses well into the nineteenth century, they grew to become books of several hundred (in extreme cases thousand) pages. For those who did not advance up the university hierarchy, a doctor's degree from the faculties of philosophy and theology qualified a person for a position as senior teacher in the schools; it was the foundation of the Swedish grammar school tradition for as long as this survived. A doctorate also opened the door to higher ecclesiastical office.

The majority of the students lived in private lodgings; these were the days of attic rooms and paraffin lamps. At the beginning of the century there were only three student hostels; buildings for the nations and large halls of residence began to be built only in the 1940s. Students usually ate in regular groups, often organized by clergymen's widows. This institution of the *matlag*, as it was called, played an important role not only for the students' daily bread; memoirs from the first decades of the twentieth century bear witness to its importance as a medium for the exchange of ideas and the formation of coteries. The strong masculine dominance in the student body persisted. In the first decade of the century there were only ten-odd female students; during the 1910s the number increased to over a hundred.

Industry was gaining ground in what had once been an agrarian village; along with industry came the growing labour movement. In 1902 the first demonstration calling for universal adult suffrage paraded through the streets of Lund to the accompaniment of the red banners of the trade unions. The few rows of students in white caps who took part naturally aroused considerable attention.

The sense of tradition in the university was strong. A symbol of oneness with past generations can be seen in the raising of busts outside the university building and in Lundagård; they represent distinguished university scholars from the eighteenth and nineteenth centuries, among them Sven Nilsson, Kilian Stobaeus, Anders Jahan Retzius, Sven Lagerbring, Otto Lindblad.

These academic forefathers, materialized in bronze, looked down upon the new generation which passed by; in this symbolic world the opposition between old and new was heightened. The undercurrents of conflict often came to the surface, in particular on three occasions concerning academic appointments, which were as much battles over academic freedom. The squabbles concerned Knut Wicksell, a member of the radical Verdandi club in Uppsala, who was applying for the post of professor of political economy; the radical Lundensian Bengt Lidforss, who was applying for the prolongation of his appointment as lecturer in botany; and the free-thinking lecturer in theology, Torgny Segerstedt, an applicant for a professorship in the history of religion.

An active part in each of these cases was played by the university vice-chancellor, Gottfrid Billing, who was bishop of Lund from 1898. He was a man of power and authority. He believed that by virtue of his office he was entitled to set the norms of the university, and therefore tried in each of these three cases to check new developments in directions of which he disapproved. (He was nonetheless known for the way he allowed himself to enliven academic celebrations with his disarming Scanian sense of humour.) Billing's intervention in promotional matters led to the ending of the vice-chancellor's power (or abuse of power) in questions of academic appointments in 1908. Later the office of vice-chancellor was also abolished. This office was in fact the last relic of the time when the university was organized on the model of Catholic monasteries, with a church dignitary at the top.

The academic world in Lund in the first decades of the century was, with a few notable exceptions, a citadel for the preservation of the social status quo. Yet it is the radical voices and opinions, heralding a future society, which have attracted most attention from historians of later decades. From the ranks of D.Y.G. came a long series of leaders for the new popular movement, the social democratic movement which was still at this time progressive.

Around the turn of the century a new generation of Lund students made their voices heard in literature. They were all anchored in the province of Scania, but with a modern and European outlook. The only one to achieve a name for

121

himself outside Sweden was Vilhelm Ekelund, who published his first poems in a student calendar in 1901. His poetry was soon translated into German; his prose aphorisms have in recent times appeared in French, German, and English versions.

The early twentieth century was a time of political strife, brought to the fore by the dissolution of the union of Sweden and Norway in 1905. The conflicts which this provoked caused echoes in the student world, with violent scenes enacted within the walls of the Academic Union.

Despite the political storms, however, the students and dons lived in a sheltered world. To be sure, it did happen that the radical professor of economics, Knut Wicksell, was sentenced to a spell in Ystad gaol in 1908. He had been convicted of blasphemy; in a speech he had poked fun at the idea of the immaculate conception. Yet in the same year the Lund carnival was held in the usual frolicking spirit. For this carnival was created the most celebrated Lund revue ever, 'Princess Uarda's Secret or The Prophecy of the Sphinx', superficially based on the historical novel *Uarda* by the German Egyptologist Georg Eber. The revue was ostensibly set in ancient Egypt, but was as much concerned with current student life.

In this carefree town the economic situation of the student was irregular, often precarious. The banks had started offering sizeable loans. There was now the chance of prolonging one's student days — without passing any exams — for a practically unlimited time. This was thus the golden age of the down-at-heel perpetual student, symbol of an irresponsible and reckless student romanticism. Living on bills of exchange could lead to disaster for both the borrowers and their guarantors. The fate of Gunnar Serner became well known throughout Sweden. After a hasty doctoral dissertation and loans of dubious legality he was forced to go into exile, later rehabilitating himself under the pen-name of Frank Heller; he lived in Casa Collina on Bornholm, where he wrote novels with Filip Collin as the leading character.

The Academic Union, the Café Tua, the Grand Hotel, and Gambrinus were the meeting places for different generations, for old and new traditions. The year 1905 saw the creation of a new institution unique to Lund: student soirées. The aim was to stimulate greater intellectual activity among the students by means of lectures, debates, and literary readings. The new tradition began with a lecture on 'The Student and the Social Question'. For the following decades and right up to the present day, student soirées have continued to play an important role in breaking isolation in the university milieu, in establishing contact between the student and the outside world, and also as a channel for European culture. Speakers and actors have been selected from widely varying groups. Generations of authors, singers, actors, and politicians have appeared:

Bertrand Russell, W.H. Auden, Maurice Chevalier, Marcel Marceau, Leni Riefensthal, Karen Blixen, and Mikis Theodorakis, to name just a few of the better-known European guests. In addition, Sweden's prime ministers have generally submitted themselves to a confrontation with each new generation of Lund students.

The mobilization in 1914 at the outbreak of the Great War, when all the church bells in Sweden tolled, marked an interruption in the life of the student town. The war led to conscription, rationing, and the so-called Bratt system, which meant a restriction of the hitherto free sales of spirits in hotels and other public places. An alcohol-saturated student epoch came to an end.

The effects of the war were not witnessed at first hand until the transports of exchanged prisoners and wounded soldiers began on the Swedish railways. The local press noted, almost as a curiosity, that the French lector in Lund had been wounded on the eastern front. The newspapers discussed with greater indignation the issue of whether the time really was appropriate for dances and balls in the Academic Union.

Neutral Sweden remained outside the conflict, but the effects of the war on academic life were felt in many ways. The Spanish flu raged in the autumn of 1918, claiming many victims. Food prices soared, and the shortage of food brought the mass of students into a critical situation. Many of the old food groups had to be dissolved. The eventual solution was the establishment of a student refectory early in 1919. Shortages made themselves felt in many areas: even the white velvet for the student caps, which had previously been imported from England, was now hard to come by.

Clever Hans and B.L.

If Tegnér and Agardh had stood side by side as the portal figures of the university in the Romantic Age, there is good reason to place at the door to the twentieth century a new humanist and a new scientist: Hans Larsson and Bengt Lidforss. Hans Larsson was a humanist with a background in natural science; Bengt Lidforss was a scientist with a broad grasp of the arts.

'Und in Skånes Hauptstadt Lund lebt auch ihr grosser, stiller, wenigen bekannter Dichterdenker.' With these words the poet Rainer Maria Rilke describes Hans Larsson in a letter to his wife. The poet-philosopher Hans Larsson was no scholarly giant and not a particularly professorial professor. He was one of those Lund University dons who came direct from agrarian society to the world of learning; the more usual direction in this academic circulation of the classes was from the plough via the pulpit to the university

The philosopher Hans Larsson at his writing-desk.

chair. Born on a farm which had been passed down in the family for several generations, Hans Larsson cautiously separated himself from the peasant tradition.

He became an independent thinker, who wandered far from his village in the company of Plato and Spinoza, of Kant and Fichte. Yet his excursions into philosophical territory never took him very far away from his native milieu, the plain of Scania and the character of its people. This professor of philosophy in Lund retained something of the peasant in his physical appearance and in his curt, thoughtful speech. He was never spoiled by the academic environment; he remained a man for whom philosophy was not merely theory, the analysis of concepts, and speculation, but also common sense and worldly wisdom. On his gravestone in Lund's northern cemetery there is a quotation from Spinoza under his name: *Bene agere et laetari* 'Act right and be joyful'.

As a student in Lund he had begun to read for a bachelor's degree in natural sciences, with a view to becoming a doctor. The new view of life revealed by biology brought to the fore for Larsson, as for many others in an entire generation, fundamental questions about life. His path to philosophy was via Darwin and Haeckel.

After a period away from Lund he returned to study for the Bachelor of Arts degree, taking history and the two philosophy examinations. During a convalescence from an attack of incipient tuberculosis, when he had gone home to the country, he wrote his *Intuition*, a work with the subtitle *Några ord om diktning och vetenskap* ('Some Words on Poetry and Science'). The book is at once a piece of introspective psychological investigation and a contribution to the theory of knowledge. He presents his view — based on his own personal experience — of intuition as a logical, synthetic form of perception common to poets, artists, and scientists.

In 1893 Hans Larsson defended his compactly written doctor's thesis, a slim but rich book about Kant's transcendental deduction of the categories. In Germany a wave of neo-Kantianism had for a time swept away Hegelianism and positivism. Hans Larsson aligned himself fully with Kant and the neo-Kantian view of consciousness as an original synthesis, anticipating and shaping experience.

In the following years as a lecturer in Lund he lectured on topics such as poetic technique from the epistemological point of view. He summarized his results in the book *Poesiens logik* ('The Logic of Poetry'). Here he pursued the line of thought first presented in his *Intuition*; he sought to show how distinctively poetic effects like metaphors, symbols, synaesthetic analogies, rhythms, all have a logical, synthetic effect.

In his lectures he chose to concentrate on fundamental questions of philosophy. Typical of these is the title of his book on Plato, which was for decades compulsory reading for all students of philosophy in Lund; *Platon och vår tid* ('Plato and Our Times') was as much an introduction to the basic problems of philosophy. Before Alfred North Whitehead he expressed his view of the history of European ideas as 'footnotes to Plato'. Hans Larsson's other main work, that on Spinoza, was also organized according to systematic rather than historical principles.

Hans Larsson became known to the general public through his articles in the daily press and his minor works of philosophical reflections. These were essays which often took as their theme current political problems or literary texts.

Students of varying subjects and with diverse political views attended his seminars, which he led with his maieutic Socratic method. The discussions took as their starting points, besides the ever-topical Plato, contemporary thinkers: the phenomenologist Husserl and the intuitive philosopher Bergson, against whom he carried on a polemic on the intuition problem in a French forum — his book on intuition quickly appeared in a French edition.

Hans Larsson was never to build up a system or found a school. He preferred to philosophize in hints; he did not want to teach a finished system, but rather a way of thinking. In this way he guided generations of Lund students.

During two world wars he stood up as an uncompromising defender of the ideas and liberal values of the constitutional state. His last public appearance in an academic gathering concerned a protest against the transport of Norwegian students to Nazi Germany. He was then in his eighties, suffering from his final illness, yet he wanted once more to speak his mind.

Hans Larsson strove to make his philosophical prose accessible and comprehensible, without terminological confusion, and the same strivings characterized his successors. It was not until the generation of the 1960s that analytical philosophy of the Anglo-Saxon model and the continental philosophical traditions found a place in Lund. The Hans Larsson tradition, with its attitude of meditation over life's philosophical questions, was probably responsible for this delay. In recent decades the opposition between analytical philosophy and the speculative tradition of Heidegger and later continental philosophy has given rise to new tensions in the subject.

A scientist whose rebellious ardour has already been glimpsed in the foregoing pages is Bengt Lidforss. Alongside Hans Larsson he had a significant influence — both positive and negative — on the climate of ideas in the Lund of his time.

He was the son of a professor and something of an academic child prodigy. Yet he had neither the desire nor the talent to play the role of a model student. He entered student life in the 1880s, a time when alcohol flowed freely and prostitutes walked the streets. He demonstrated his quick wit in the academic debating societies. He made the acquaintance of Strindberg, who was in Lund in 1890. He found his way into the Tua coterie, that extravagant, bacchanalian intelligentsia with its airs of Nietzscheanism. Areschough, the profesor of biology, quickly made him a research assistant in his department and stimulated his interest in the genus *Rubus*. Lidforss continued his studies of plant physiology, partly in Lund, partly in Germany, with famous mentors like Wilhelm Pfeffer and Ernst Stahl. He was drawn into the Bohemian life of the Scandinavian artists in Berlin, whose regular haunt was the pub *Zum schwarzen Ferkel*. Edvard Munch and August Strindberg were among the leading figures there. After several years of this stormy German odyssey he returned like the prodigal son to his parental home in Lund, where he — in the daytime — continued his research, took his doctorate, and became a lecturer under the stern Areschough.

His combination of a Bohemian life-style, an intractable radicalism, and a later open commitment to the labour movement was a thorn in the flesh to the fathers of the academic establishment. His opinions led to downright persecution from the chancellor and vice-chancellor of the university. Lidforss, one of the sharpest polemists in the whole of Swedish literature, did not mince his words in his attacks on the academic authorities and the conservative atmosphere of his home town.

As a botanist he pursued research in various spheres, working on plants and their resistance to frost, on pollen biology, and on evergreen plants. He was best known, however, for his experiments in plant physiology, which were significant as the first analysis of an entire plant genus in which specific properties were demonstrated to follow Mendel's laws.

Lidforss' projected major work on the genus *Rubus* was never completed. His life and his research were stunted by setbacks of various kinds, interruptions and distractions in his work, the incurable disease which he had contracted in his early years. A thirteen-page summary in the *Zeitschrift für induktive Abstammungs- und Vererbungslehre*, completed only a few days before the haemorrhage which led to his death, was to be the final chapter of his scholarly work.

Lidforss has been acclaimed or decried above all as a spokesman for radical culture and ideology, as a man of contradictions in the history of ideas in Lund. He showed a remarkable fixation with Christianity, although he had liberated himself from religion during a painful adolescent crisis. His last and greatest book, finished towards the end of his life, is entitled *Kristendomen förr och nu* ('Christianity Past and Present'). He was convinced that the new liberal theology in Germany had dealt the death blow to Christianity. He sought a replacement for Christian faith in the theory of evolution. Darwinism led him to view the cosmos with a mysticism which at times approached a religious awe.

Lidforss thus has his place in history for his research in botany and for his contentious views on the philosophy of life. Yet he also has a place in the history of politics and literature. His cultural and geopolitical perspective was Scanian and pro-German, sometimes with a hazardous dash of the anti-Semitism which was common in his day. No one has been portrayed so often — whether with repulsion or admiration — in the gallery of novels and memoirs from Lund.

On Bengt Lidforss' grave in the cemetery of St Peter's Monastery grow the thorny tendrils of bramble bushes, genus *Rubus*.

Axel Herrlin and the new psychology

In his younger years Axel Herrlin belonged to the same group as Hans Larsson and Bengt Lidforss. His academic destination was the newly established chair of psychology and education.

Axel Herrlin was something of an academic shooting star. He was only twenty-two years old when he defended his doctoral dissertation on the Renaissance philosopher Nicholas of Cusa. He then went on to write a larger work in the history of philosophy, dealing with Renaissance ethics, where he followed leads from Burckhardt and other contemporary Renaissance scholars. He was appointed to oppose Hans Larsson's doctoral dissertation on Kant, but he was passed over when together with Larsson he applied for the professorship in philosophy.

Alongside his studies in the history of philosophy he oriented himself in psychology. This had evolved as an experimental science in Europe around 1870. It was then that Wilhelm Wundt at Leipzig University founded the first psychological laboratory and developed experimental methods closely connected to the modern physiology of the day. Axel Herrlin himself studied experimental psychology with another German representative of the new subject, G.E. Müller in Göttingen, as well as with Alfred Lehmann in his celebrated laboratory in Copenhagen. This schooling imbued him in a view of science which was to all intents and purposes positivist.

Towards the end of the nineteenth century there was a growing interest in marginal psychological phenomena such as dreams, hallucinations, and hypnotic states; this occasionally went hand in hand with an interest in occultism and spiritism. Strindberg had lively discussions about dreams and occult phenomena with his Lundensian friends in the medical faculty and with Herrlin, who actually kept private notes on his own dreams. In a book called *Själslivets underjordiska värld* ('The Subterranean World of the Mind'), published in 1901, he was the first in Sweden to treat the unconscious mind in a scientific study. He showed that he was thoroughly familiar with Eduard von Hartmann and the French psychologist Pierre Janet, but that he as yet knew nothing of Sigmund Freud.

Herrlin had a gigantic memory, with a polymath's thirst for knowledge, covering vast regions of the arts and sciences alike; his own memoirs from Lund in the 1880s are one of the most frequently cited contemporary sources. He was one of the last to exemplify an age when a broad knowledge of philosophy and the humanities could go hand in hand with a thorough grounding in scientific thought and experimental methodology.

Lund theology

At the beginning of the century the faculty of theology had six professors, with a seventh chair added in the 1910s. A statute of 1903 ruled that the examination for the Bachelor of Theology degree should consist of a theoretical part and a practical part, the latter occupying one term. The faculty had a special place in the university thanks to its connection with the state church system. From the earliest days of the university it had been considered self-evident that those responsible for the education of the clergy should themselves be ordained clergymen.

The six professorships still had their prebendaryships. The question of whether this system should continue or not was discussed over many decades, and various arguments, both financial and theological, were heard. It was not until the 1940s that the last vestiges of the system disappeared. Yet long before this, the question of whether professors of theology should be confessionally orthodox was raised by the nomination of Torgny Segerstedt for the new chair of the history of religion.

At the start of the century Swedish theology had received new signals from — as so often before — Germany. Theological circles there had shown concern and dismay in the 1870s when Julius Wellhausen, in his famous *Prolegomena*, treated the books of the Old Testament with the critical, genetic, and historical method hitherto reserved for profane literature. This marked the definitive break with the old doctrine of the divine inspiration of the scriptures. Influenced by the secularizing trend in Imperial Germany, Albrecht Ritschl and Adolf von Harnack developed a theology where the supernatural message was set aside in favour of a historical view of the Bible, with emphasis on Christian ethics and practical religion.

This liberal German theology also enjoyed a certain success in Lund, although the faculty had a strong conservative phalanx. As the contemporary philosophers in Lund were returning to Kant, so the theologians sought support in Luther. Two of them, Pehr Eklund and Magnus Pfannenstill, were active less as writers than as oral preachers and debaters in the controversial disputes about Christianity which were raging; in skirmishes in the Academic Union their chief opponent was the new spokesman of the scientific philosophy of life, Bengt Lidforss.

Research in religion was given an empirical direction, beyond confessional orthodoxy, in the field of comparative religion which emerged towards the end of the nineteenth century, with its historical and ethnographical orientation. It was in this subject that the young Torgny Segerstedt defended his doctoral dissertation on the origin of polytheism; he then became a lecturer in the subject. He had spent his early years as a student in Germany, where he had attended Adolf von Harnack's lectures. Influenced as he was by liberal theology, by his own studies of religion as well as of Søren Kierkegaard, he had a more liberal and radical attitude to Christianity than his colleagues in the faculty. He had even expressed a certain sympathy for Bengt Lidforss' criticism of Christianity. It was proposed by the liberal wing in the theology faculty that Segerstedt be appointed to the new professorship in the history of religion, even though he was not ordained. The experts unanimously recommended him for the chair, but the faculty rejected him by a slender majority. The battle for this professorship has been called the last deadly serious debate on the principle of scholarly freedom in Sweden. Segerstedt withdrew his application and was given a donation professorship in the faculty of arts at Stockholm College. He did not remain there for long, but continued his career as a liberal journalist, in time becoming the newspaper world's most vigorous assailant of Nazi Germany and the most energetic defender of human and humanist values.

A scholar who enjoyed Scandinavian and international recognition was called on to fill the empty chair in Segerstedt's place: Edvard Lehmann. He came from a famous Danish family and had as a young man studied in Lund, thanks to an Oehlenschläger-Tegnér scholarship. In Lund he had come into close contact with Pehr Eklund. He was one of the first Danes since the time of the first university in the seventeenth century to become a professor in Lund, to where he was called after occupying the first chair in the subject of comparative religion in Berlin.

He had studied and done research in Germany, France, and England. Two teachers who had a powerful influence on his scholarly outlook were the German philologist Hermann Usener and the Dutch theologian and historian of religion Chantepie de la Saussaye. Lehmann's major scholarly work is a book on Zarathustra; his other writings included studies of Indian and Persian religion. With his inventive wit he was an important figure in academic life on many fronts, among other things as a journalist and essayist. A rich array of anecdotes bear witness to his talent for irony, often at his own expense. One story tells how he once introduced himself to a travelling salesman on the ferry to Copenhagen: 'I'm a travelling salesman too,' he declared; 'I sell articles of faith.'

The specific concept of 'Lund theology' has since the 1930s come to denote above all the work and ideas of two professors, Anders Nygren and Gustaf Aulén. The elder of the two was Aulén. He came from Uppsala to succeed Pehr Eklund as professor of systematic theology (dogmatics). In his largest work, *Den allmänna kristna tron* (translated as *The Faith of the Christian Church*), which was used as a textbook for decades both in Scandinavia and elsewhere, he gave his interpretation of the content and meaning of Christian faith. Referring frequently to contemporary English and German theology, his emphasis on dualism in Christian doctrine brings him close to Luther; he depicts as a drama both the individual's struggle for life and the course of world events in a Christian perspective.

After his years as Bishop of Strängnäs, Aulén returned in 1952 to Lund, where he continued to write about theology with a contemporary emphasis. Fascinated by Dag Hammarskjöld's personality and his fate as Secretary General of the United Nations, he wrote an English commentary to Hammarskjöld's 'white book' *Markings*, with its strain of Christian mysticism. He devoted one of his last books to modern research into the figure of Jesus. Back in the 1920s he had been one of the founders of *Svensk Teologisk Kvartalskrift*, a periodical which did long service as an organ for Lund theology.

The foremost of the Lund theologians was undeniably Anders Nygren. His basic schooling was in German philosophy and theology, but not the liberal German school of Harnack which continued along the path of romantic idealism; Nygren's work was in large part a challenge to this tradition. The title of his doctoral dissertation, *Religiöst apriori* ('Religious Apriorism'), indicates his neo-Kantian trend. Nygren presents in the book the opinion which he maintained through the years, namely that there is a universal, specific religious form of experience of an atheoretical sort, a religious 'category' in the Kantian sense. In a succession of other works he examined questions on the boundary between philosophy and theology. Using a systematic and historical method, he sought to establish the fundamental nature of Christianity, its individuality and its historical forms. This was the subject of his greatest work, *Den kristna kärlekstanken genom tiderna, eros och agape* (translated as *Eros and Agape: A Study of the Christian Idea of Love*), which appeared in two parts between 1930 and 1936.

No theological work by a Swedish scholar has attracted the same international attention as this book. It was translated not only into a large number of European languages but also into Chinese and Japanese. Nygren here contrasted two basic motifs. One of these, *eros*, derives from Plato and idealistic philosophy; the other, *agape*, has its origin in the New Testament. The struggle and the compromises between these two motifs, that of self-perfection and that of self-effacing love, run throughout the course of Christian history, from the earliest days to the Renaissance. According to Nygren's exposition, it was not until Luther that the 'synthesis' was finally dissolved, and Christianity was restored to its purity and individuality. For both Nygren and Aulén, 'Lund theology' was a rediscovery of Luther; the same is true of the third of the leading Lund theologists, Ragnar Bring.

Hans Larsson raised a cautious philosopher's objections to Nygren's sharp distinction of the two motifs, and to the absolute demarcation line between

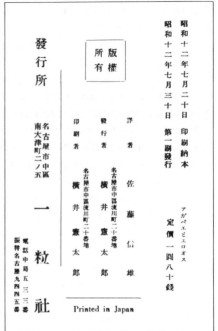

Title pages of Anders Nygren's Eros and Agape, *the first Swedish edition and the Japanese translation.*

Christianity and Platonism. Theological critics of Nygren's work included one of his pupils and his successor as professor, Gustaf Wingren. In a work on questions of theological methodology (translated as *Theology in Conflict: Nygren, Barth, Bultmann*), he commented on Nygren's *magnum opus* from historical and methodological points of view. Gustaf Wingren himself is known for his work on medieval theology and on Luther's concept of vocation; his own basic views of theology laid a strong emphasis on the role of creation.

Anders Nygren's last major book was an attempt to provide a scientific foundation for the discipline of systematic theology, on the basis of typological or structural research into motifs. The work is entitled *Meaning and Method: Prolegomena to a Scientific Philosophy of Religion and a Scientific Theology* (1972). By the word 'scientific' he sought to emphasize the use of objective argument, by which theology strove for the same exactness as the natural sciences. The book is a defence of theology in a 'neo-positivist' age. In it he poses the questions: 'How is a philosophy as a science possible?' and 'How is theology as a science possible?' He confronts Paul Tillich and Rudolf

Bultmann in their proclaimed intention of 'demythologizing' Christianity. At the same time he returns to the Kantian 'categorial' perspective of his youth. The book is thus Nygren's last contribution to the century-long debate on the position of theology within or outside the system of the recognized sciences. It takes into account new ideas from linguistic philosophy, including Wittgenstein, and with reference to the different contexts of meaning where various types of statement can be considered to belong.

Nygren had a dominant influence on his colleagues and pupils, who wrote historically oriented dissertations on systematic theology. Outside the narrow confines of the discipline, traces of his theology can be discerned even in contemporary literature.

Towards the middle of the century, theological research in Lund had taken on a largely historical bias. Exegetes worked with the philological methods of contemporary linguistic research; younger generations of church historians had the same critical approach to their sources as secular historians. In the faculty of theology, where Henrik Reuterdahl had once raised ecclesiastical history to the status of a scientific subject, the history of the Swedish church from the Middle Ages to the nineteenth century has been the object of considerable research and examination from new angles. Close collaboration with ethnologists and social scientists has led to the foundation of Kyrkohistoriska Folklivsarkivet, an interdisciplinary archive collecting material on old folk customs associated with the church in the south of Sweden.

The restructuring of theological studies after the new university reforms has had the effect of reducing the amount of linguistic and historical matter taught in the faculty, and with it the textual study of the Bible. New fields oriented to the modern function of theology in society have given rise to new professorships (philosophy of religion and sociology of religion); there is also teaching in the psychology of religion. The closed world of classical 'Lund theology' in the 1930s has been exploded, giving way to the study of belief in a more pluralistic spirit. The creation of a chair of Islamology in the 1980s marks a tendency to direct research and teaching towards new areas of politico-religious importance. The theology faculty, dominated from the earliest days by men, has shown a changed face in recent decades. In the 1980s more than half of the students in the theology faculty are women. This has to do with the church reform of 1958 which gave women the right to be ordained. The final practical training for clergy in the Church of Sweden is nowadays provided by a special Pastoral Institute, separate from the theology faculty.

Leading lights in the faculty of law

At the beginning of the century the number of professors responsible for teaching and examining the various subjects in the faculty of law was seven. Two of them distinguish themselves from the others by their eccentricity: Johan C. W. Thyrén and Knut Wicksell.

In the winters towards the close of the nineteenth century it was possible to observe a remarkable sight at the Lund sports ground: a thirty-year-old professor on skates, dressed in topcoat and top hat. This was Johan C. W. Thyrén, professor of criminal law, polymath, orator, active athlete (in which property he was duly elected chairman when Lund University Gymnastics and Sports Association (LUGI) was founded in 1912). Moreover, he soon attracted countless anecdotes, not all of them decent.

He had an early initiation into the faculty of law through his maternal grandfather, Carl Johan Schlyter, editor of the medieval laws of Sweden. His academic career was meteoric. Doctor of philosophy at the age of 22 with a dissertation on Herbert Spencer's psychology, his first appointment was as lecturer in philosophy for three years, after which a new dissertation qualified him for a lectureship in history for eight years. His lectures in this subject drew a multifarious audience. For a time he also had well-advanced plans to become professor of aesthetics. In the end, however, he opted for law. After deputizing in the subjects of Roman law and history of law, in 1896 he became professor of criminal law, at the age of 35. When he left this in 1926, he had also been university rector for ten years.

Thyrén's most important work was as a theoretician and a reformer of criminal law. His early dissertation in German on causality — the question of criminal intent versus negligence — aroused a certain interest outside Sweden. In the 1890s he became a member of the Internationale Kriminalistische Vereinigung in Berlin, which represented the sociological school in criminal law. It was headed by Franz von Liszt, who regarded crime as primarily a social problem and saw it as the role of punishment to deter, improve, and prevent.

One task assigned to Thyrén by the government was to prepare a reform of Swedish criminal law. His proposals show how close he was to the sociological school, although through time he developed his own variant of this tendency. He published a three-volume proposed programme, *Principerna för en straff-lagsreform* ('Principles for a Reform of Criminal Law'). This was followed by circumstantial and comprehensive historical and comparative studies of the forms of crime and punishment in various cultures, European, Asiatic, African. During his lifetime he saw the introduction of two reforms which he had advocated: the abolition of the death penalty in 1921, and automatic psychiatric examination of people accused of certain types of crime.

Thyrén was elected to parliament at the beginning of the century. For a short period in the 1920s he served in the government as minister of justice. In all his roles, as member of parliament, as professor, as rector, he impressed people with his studied, effective rhetoric.

Of a quite different temperament was Thyrén's colleague in the faculty of law, the professor of political economy and financial law, Knut Wicksell. During his radical youth in Uppsala, when he was in contact with Hjalmar Branting, one of the pioneers of social democracy, with August Strindberg and Georg Brandes, he had instructed himself in a subject new for the times, political economy. On visits to England and the continent he read works by leading men in the scientific study of economics, among them the Austrian E. von Böhm-Bawerk, whose theory of capital and marginal utility were something of a revelation to Wicksell. He further developed the theories, applying strictly mathematical methods.

He saw political economy as essentially the study of quantities: 'What cannot here be expressed in mathematical form is in fact not an object of our knowledge, but mere playing with words,' he wrote in the draft to an introduction to his first major work, *Über Wert, Kapital und Rente*. This and two other innovative books in German made him the virtual founder of Swedish political economy.

As a member of the radical Verdandi club in Uppsala he had gained the reputation of being a dangerous subversive. In his public contributions to the debate on population he had used Malthusian ideas about the poverty which threatened Sweden as a result of over-population to support his plea for birth control and family planning. It was also known that he was living in a common-law marriage without the blessing of the church. Could such a man become professor in Lund?

When the matter of his application came up before the Consistory, there was criticism, from theologians among others, of his views and their presumed effect on the young people he would be teaching. But the majority of the Consistory voted to follow the experts who had declared him best qualified for the chair. Gottfrid Billing, the bishop and vice-chancellor, vetoed the appointment. The threat to academic freedom which Billing's objection constituted provoked a petition of protest signed by more than half of the student body. When the matter came to a higher authority, Wicksell was recommended by the university chancellor and was appointed by the king in council.

A contemporary Lundensian, the linguist and politician Ernst Wigforss, writing his memoirs after World War II, commented on the events in a historical perspective:

Wicksell received his professorship. Fifty years ago. So deeply rooted in bourgeois society had ideas of academic freedom, the doctrinal freedom of the scholar, become. Imagine as consistent and ruthless an opponent of prevailing ideologies today; in which countries would he be appointed professor or not, to say nothing of where he would or would not be allowed to live?

Once appointed to his chair, Wicksell held a series of lectures on political economy, in the first of which he treated pricing, production, and distribution, in the second money and credit systems. The lectures were a systematic exposition of the theories he had already developed in his German works. The lectures, which were so difficult that when published they were called a textbook for professors, have appeared in German, English, Spanish, and Italian, the latter translation published as late as 1950. They have played a role in international economic discussion; concepts such as excess purchasing power and the inflationary gap, important for later economic theory, can be derived from Wicksell's analyses and monetary theory. As late as 1986, the winner of the Nobel Prize for economics, James Buchanan, acknowledged the stimulus of Wicksell's early writings.

Even after his retirement Wicksell was active as a debater on social issues and as a consultant to the Bank of Sweden. It was with a travel grant from the Bank of Sweden back in February 1916 that he had met (probably the first Swede to do so) J.M. Keynes and his colleagues in Cambridge; Wicksell described Keynes as 'their sharpest theoretician'. As he wrote to his wife, 'We had a very interesting conversation. He was not so well versed in every point. ... I only wish we had had more time.'

A colleague of both Thyrén and Wicksell was Ernst Kallenberg, professor of procedural law from 1897. As with Thyrén, the German school exerted a strong influence on Kallenberg, whose authorities included the Berlin professor Konrad Hellweg and the Leipzig professor Oskar Bülow, the former a specialist in procedural law, the latter an innovator in the field of civil law. Kallenberg's monumental work, *Svensk civilprocessrätt* ('Swedish Civil Procedural Law'), is modelled on Hellweg's huge *System des deutschen Zivilprozessgericht*. This work made him the great name in the doctrine of procedure in the first decades of the twentieth century.

A later generation of legal scholars in Lund took a new theoretical direction under the leadership of Karl Olivecrona. His view of law bore the stamp of his master, Axel Hägerström, professor of practical philosophy in Uppsala. By analysing and revealing the religious and metaphysical strains in legal thought from Roman times until the present day, Hägerström became the founder of the Scandinavian school of legal realism. It was his ambition and that of his successors to raise the study of law from the level of speculation to a science. Terms like 'rights' and 'guilt', still much used by Thyrén in his *Principles for a Reform of Criminal Law*, were to be abandoned because of their irrational and unscientific overtones.

Olivecrona, professor of procedural law in Lund from 1933, further developed Hägerström's ideas. He saw legal rules as rules for behaviour, whose force is not derived from metaphysical or religious ideas but from their acceptance by citizens, judges, and public officials, ultimately because of the power of the state in organizing society. The harsh title of his best-known work is *Law as Fact*, the English edition of which appeared in 1939; it was translated into German two years later as *Gesetz und Staat*.

The fundamental outlook of the book when it was published made it better suited to countries controlled with the force which characterized Hitler's Third Reich or Franco's Spain (where the book also appeared in translation) than for western democracies. Olivecrona, unable to see what had been lost when the legal system of the Weimar Republic was abolished, stubbornly supported Nazi Germany from his ivory tower.

Olivecrona saw himself exclusively as a scholar; he was not tempted by public duties in the field of legislation or the administration of justice. The reverse was true of Hjalmar Karlgren, professor of civil law and international civil law in the 1930s and 1940s. As a legal scholar he was typical of his times, devoting his years in Lund to research in the law of contracts and torts. He had studied this subject under the foremost German authorities, but he regarded as his true forerunners the Danish legal scientists Julius Lassen and Henry Ussing. In 1946 he was appointed Justice of the Supreme Court. While serving as a judge he also wrote extensively on matters of jurisprudence. He has been described as one of the keenest brains ever to come from the faculty of law in Lund.

From the 1960s there has been a certain change in the research profile and the teaching structure of the faculty. One line of development has been along the boundary with the growing descriptive and analytical social sciences. Another has been connected with the modern linguistic science of meaning, semantics. At the same time, the classical spheres of law have by and large maintained their position.

Among the linguists

The time up to World War II was a favourable climate for the humanities. The goals and methods of research and teaching long continued to follow the traditions of nineteenth-century humanism. This applies not least to linguistics. In an earlier era, before the turn of the century, linguistic scholars in Lund had been chiefly occupied in producing instruments for the understanding of language and literature — they had been lexicographers or translators.

The new generation of linguists in the twentieth century were all specialists in their own fields, prepared to make historical and comparative contributions to the linguistics of their day. They have mostly been interested in earlier stages of language, whether they have been historical linguists, etymologists, or editors of texts.

The prevailing school in German linguistics in the late nineteenth century called themselves *Junggrammatiker* (Neogrammarians). Their ideal was the approach of the natural sciences: the search for laws, the demand for exact empirical observation, and the distaste for loose philosophical speculation.

During his years of study in Germany in the 1870s, the young Axel Kock from Lund had established close contact with representatives of the current school of historical linguistics, from whom he had acquired his view of the subject. In his doctoral dissertation he wrote about Swedish accent, investigating the origin of the tones and their significance for historical phonology. In 1907 he filled the vacant chair of Scandinavian languages. A few years later he was elected rector of the university.

During his years in Lund he wrote a huge work summarizing the historical phonology of Swedish, *Svensk ljudhistoria*, which appeared in five parts between 1906 and 1929. In it he treats the history of the Swedish vowels, setting up rules for umlaut and breaking, with constant comparison of corresponding phenomena in the other Scandinavian languages. Here as in his other work, he shows himself as a meticulous observer of details and strict methods.

Axel Kock was a master for all those studying the history of the Scandinavian languages in his time. His interest also included the modern dialects; he planned the systematic surveys of the dialects of Southern Sweden which were later organized by the Dialect (and now also Place-Name) Archive in Lund.

In the same year as Axel Kock was nominated professor in Lund, one of his younger contemporaries also became professor: Elof Hellquist. He was a pupil of Adolf Noreen in Uppsala and, like Kock, he was close to the Neogrammarian school in his approach to linguistic phenomena. Hellquist came to Lund in 1914 to occupy a newly established second chair of Scandinavian languages. His main interests were word formation and etymology. His best-known work is his etymological dictionary, *Svensk etymologisk ordbok*, published between 1920 and 1922, still an indispensable reference work after sixty years.

Another student of the earlier stages of language was Axel Kock's cousin, Ernst Albin Kock. In 1906 he became the first occupant of a chair of German in Lund. His initial work was devoted to the textual criticism and editing of early English and German texts. He later came to specialize chiefly in Old Icelandic poetry. He based his textual interpretations on comparisons of Old Norse phraseology and idiom with evidence in the other Germanic languages, especially the Anglo-Saxon poetic monuments. His comparative method and his results brought him into violent conflict with the older school of Icelandic scholarship, represented by Finnur Jónsson in Copenhagen. In the over three thousand sections of his *Notationes Norrœnæ*, annotations to Eddic and skaldic poetry, he examined passages which he reinterpreted according to his own, often bold, ideas. He thought that he had initiated something of a revolution in his view of the Icelandic skaldic poems and their value as historical sources. A posthumous edition of the entire skaldic corpus incorporated all the emendations which he had proposed on the basis of his rigid principles.

Around 1910 there was a somewhat younger group of linguists with the ambition of giving Lund a place of European rank in contemporary scholarship. The group included Eilert Ekwall, Emanuel Walberg, Einar Löfstedt, and Axel Moberg.

Ekwall had received his philological training from Adolf Noreen in Uppsala. In Lund he became the first professor in English as an independent subject. One result of his research into the history of the English language was a textbook used in many countries, *Historische neuenglische Laut- und Formenlehre* (translated as *A History of Modern English Sounds and Morphology*), of which the first edition appeared in 1914. But it was as a place-name scholar that he did his pioneering work. Trips to England every summer made him familiar with the geography and history of the individual counties. This gave him a sure topographical basis for his studies of English place-names. Through skilful etymology he was able to isolate Celtic and Scandinavian elements in the names; his findings were thus of considerable significance for the picture of England's older cultural history and the study of Viking society and settlement.

He became vice-president of the English Place-Name Society, and was in close contact with Mawer and Stenton, who had founded the society in 1924. In 1936 he published a synthesis of his toponymic research in his great reference work *The Concise Oxford Dictionary of English Place-Names*, of which the first edition has been succeeded by three revisions.

Ekwall had a long career. In his emeritus days he studied medieval London, its street-names and personal names, its settlement and population history, and its role in the establishment of a standard English language. The meticulous professor from Lund was a welcome guest among his English colleagues; he received an honorary doctorate from Oxford and was elected to the British

THE CONCISE
OXFORD DICTIONARY OF
ENGLISH
PLACE-NAMES

BY
EILERT EKWALL

FOURTH EDITION

OXFORD
AT THE CLARENDON PRESS
1960

Eilert Ekwall (1877–1965), a pioneer in onomastic research, and the title page of his dictionary of English place-names.

Academy. From his seminars came a long series of doctoral dissertations, mostly on the subject of English toponymy; he had himself provided models in his books on *The Place-Names of Lancashire* and *English River-Names*.

The strictly linguistic bias in English studies lasted until 1963, when a second chair specializing in English literature was established.

The work of Ekwall's colleague Emanuel Walberg, professor of Romance Languages, was of equally high international importance. On study trips during his youth he made contact with the leading Romance philologists of the day, Gaston Paris and Paul Meyer in Paris, and Wendelin Förster in Bonn; letters preserved in the Bibliothèque Nationale bear witness to these links. Like his masters, Walberg directed his energy towards medieval French literature, editing and commenting texts. His editions range from *Le Bestiare de Philippe de Thaün*, his 1900 doctoral dissertation, and *La Vie de Saint Thomas le Martyr* — with its account of the murder of Thomas Becket in Canterbury Cathedral — up to his edition of *Le Tombel de Chartrose*, published in 1946. He also issued a small work on the principles and methods for editing ancient texts, partly in polemic against Joseph Bédier.

140

Walberg was a learned, reserved man of the world, something of a continental type. He was equally at home on the Quai Voltaire in Paris as in the quiet avenue in Lund where his study looked out over the treetops. Like Ekwall, he received considerable recognition abroad, including the title of *associé étranger* at the Institut de France, a rare honour for a foreigner.

Another member of the European community of philologists was Axel Moberg, one of the foremost Semitists of his time. In Berlin he was encouraged by the German orientalist Karl Eduard Sachau to study closely the Syrian grammars of the thirteenth century. The result was a critical edition based on a comprehensive collection of manuscripts, *Le Livre des Splendeurs*, Moberg's major work of scholarship. A previously unknown manuscript, discovered in the fragment of a cover in a private Swedish library, was identified by him and edited with a commentary. He thus continued the Lund tradition of scholarship in oriental languages, which had been started by men like Mathias Norberg and Karl Johan Tornberg. On the administrative side, Moberg was also chairman of the Academic Union for a number of years, after which he was rector of the university for a long period. As professor of Semitic languages he was succeeded by Sven Dedering, one of the foremost Arabists of his generation, co-editor of the periodical *Le monde oriental*.

The circle of linguists in Lund was brightened by the colourful presence of the Slavonic scholar Per Sigurd Agrell. His special subject was the Polish language, but he also published studies of aspect and aktionsart in the Slavic verb and the problem of accent in the Slavonic languages. Yet he was soon bewitched by Nordic runic magic. In books with titles like *Der Ursprung der Runenschrift und die Magie* he presented his interpretation of the Scandinavian runes. In his view they originated in late antiquity, created by Germanic soldiers in the Roman legions on the model of Latin cursive script. From the mystery religions of late antiquity, in particular the Mithras cult, came the symbolism of the runic letters and their use in magic. Runes had numerical values and initially their function was chiefly magical. Agrell's bold interpretations of runic inscriptions aroused both admiration and scepticism. A scholar, a Tolstoy translator, a society genius, the sight and sound of Agrell enriched existence in Lund at the beginning of the century and for many years to come.

As has been seen, the representatives of foreign language study were, almost without exception, oriented towards research into earlier stages of language, in keeping with German and French philological tradition. The same goals and the same methodological framework sufficed for many of the succeeding generation of scholars. Erik Rooth, professor of German from 1932, worked within the paradigm of historical linguistics; in the spirit of the Neogrammarians, he followed models like Conrad Borchling and Agathe Lasch. Rooth's special field was Middle Low German; much of his work was published in *Niederdeutsches Jahrbuch* and in the series which he himself founded, Niederdeutsche Mitteilungen. The special profile which he gave to the German department was continued by another generation of his pupils, who likewise concentrated on the study of Middle Low German.

By contrast, Alf Lombard, professor of Romance languages from 1939, favoured the study of modern speech; besides research into modern French syntax, he devoted a number of works to Romanian, including *La langue roumaine* and *Dictionnaire morphologique de la langue roumaine*.

From the 1940s there was a break away from the older traditions of historical linguistics. The study of old texts and earlier stages of language receded. This did not mean that the diachronic bias had outplayed its role, but rather that it was no longer as productive and dominant. A new view of language had been developed at the beginning of the century by the Swiss linguist Ferdinand de Saussure. He and his successors emphasized the character of language as a synchronic system. The way the new semiological and structural linguistics took root in Lund can be illustrated by the career of Bertil Malmberg. As a pupil of Emanuel Walberg he had obtained his doctorate with an edition of a medieval French text. He continued with phonetic and phonological studies of modern French and other Romance languages, and in 1950 he became professor in the newly established chair of phonetics. Stimulated by Saussure, by the Hjelmslev circle of linguists in Copenhagen, and by the Russian-American structuralist Roman Jakobson, he began more and more to devote himself to the study of language as a system of signs. He left the chair of phonetics to take up a newly created chair of general linguistics, which replaced an earlier professorship of comparative Indo-European linguistics.

The revival of classical antiquity

In Europe the study of classical antiquity experienced a period of growth in the late nineteenth century and the early twentieth, combining the traditional interest in ancient texts with the new discoveries of archaeology. The intensive research carried on in Europe at the time was considered justification for the treatment of classical archaeology as an independent subject. Or, as a report from Lund University expressed it in 1908:

> Schliemann's discovery of the pre-Homeric age at Troy, Tiryns, and Mycenae has only now been properly illuminated, with the discovery in the early years of this

century of the centre of ancient culture in Crete, primarily by Arthur Evans. In Rome the methodical investigation of the Forum has given highly significant results. This has not only revealed the appearance of the Forum in its golden age and later, but also under the republic; indeed, it has taken us back to the earliest history of Rome and even beyond.

The first occupant of the chair of classical archaeology and ancient history was Martin P:n Nilsson. The year was 1909. Nine years previously he had attained the rank of lecturer in Greek with a dissertation — written in Latin — on the Greek feasts of Dionysus, *Studia de Dionysiis Atticis*. A few years later he published a continuation of this research, this time in German: *Griechische Feste von religiöser Bedeutung*. This is an attempt to determine the nature of the religious festivals of the Greeks in their historical context, on the basis of the then available evidence, whether literary, epigraphic, or archaeological. When interpreting the meaning of the cults he applied the comparative method, looking at rites and customs from other primitive agrarian cultures, including the traditions with which he had grown up in a peasant region of Scania where relics of ancient folkways had been preserved. *Griechische Feste* was the first work to make him internationally famous.

In the 1890s Martin Nilsson had studied in Basel and Berlin, establishing bonds with leading philologists of the day, Jacob Wackernagel, Hermann Diels, and Ulrich von Wilamowitz-Moellendorff, contacts which he maintained throughout the years. He continued his research, concentrating on the religious significance of the Greek festive calendar, in connection with which he studied time-reckoning and its origin in astronomical observations and the yearly round of seasonal tasks. The results were presented in works like *Primitive Time-Reckoning*. His familiarity with the rhythm of the peasant year also provided the background for a book which became a classic of Swedish ethnology, *Årets folkliga fester* ('Folk Festivals of the Year').

Later on Martin Nilsson's interests came to centre on the new region which had been unearthed by Sir Arthur Evans's excavations in Crete. The religious beliefs of the Minoans and Mycenaeans, in so far as they could be interpreted from their cult sites, buildings, pictures, and objects of various types, as well as from later myths and traditions, were the subject of *The Minoan-Mycenaean Religion and its Survivals in Greek Religion*, one of Martin Nilsson's most important works on the history of Greek religion.

In his work on Homer and Mycenae he sought to distinguish the various cultural strata in the Homeric tales, in which certain elements are traced back to the pre-literary Bronze Age. He follows the traditions down to the day when the putative poet Homer took them and moulded them into the two heroic epics

143

of the *Iliad* and the *Odyssey*; in Homeric research his stance is closest to that traditionally called the unitarian.

Much of his earlier work on the history of religion and folklife had borne the stamp of German scholarship, from his first teachers in *Altertumskunde* and from ethnographers like Mannhardt. In later years he came closer to the rather more sober Anglo-Saxon scholarship. Many of his later works were written in English; he lectured in English in the 1920s and 1930s in London, Oxford, Cambridge, and Berkeley.

During his richly productive emeritus years he returned to the history of religion, writing for a German series the two volumes of *Geschichte der griechischen Religion*. In these he summarized his lifelong research on the primitive origin of Greek religion, on the patriotic myth, on the types of procession in Greek cult, on the Eleusinian mysteries, on the influence of oriental religions in Hellenistic times. As a whole his work, characterized as it is both by his times and by his personality, represents one of the greatest, perhaps *the* greatest, achievements of the humanities in Lund in our century.

It was on his initiative that the Swedish Institute in Rome was founded, to be a centre for all later Swedish research on Italian soil. He also tried his administrative capabilities as university rector for the three years up to his retirement in 1939.

Classical archaeology, with this solid foundation provided by Martin Nilsson, was to continue to exert a strong attraction on new generations of students. The foremost of Nilsson's pupils, Axel W. Persson, had like his master taken his doctorate in Greek. He led the Swedish expedition to Asine in 1922 and the excavations in Dendra. The latter resulted in one of the most remarkable finds of later years from the Mycenaean epoch: the royal grave of Dendra. At the time of this expedition Axel W. Persson was already a professor in Uppsala. He presented the results of his research in works which were still — typically for the time — written in German.

In a later generation the most successful classical archaeologist was Martin Nilsson's successor, Einar Gjerstad. In the inter-war years he led the great expedition to Cyprus, in which King Gustav VI Adolf participated in the planning and the execution. Gjerstad is the only archaeologist of non-Italian extraction to have been granted permission in modern times to undertake excavations in Rome's most classical soil, Forum Romanum. Decade-long research in the archaeology and history of the city of Rome led to his great — and still controversial — six-volume work *Early Rome*.

In modern times classical archaeology, like Scandinavian archaeology, has been renewed through new strategies in close collaboration with scientific methods of analysis and the approach of human geography. Attitudes have also changed, so that interest is now directed not so much at the finds of individual monuments as at a broader spectrum which seeks to illuminate collective society in the past. In a time of university reforms, when the historical subjects are being set aside, classical archaeology has been able to survive by changing its name; it is now known as the culture and society of antiquity. Classical archaeology and history have thus been temporarily rescued by being metamorphosed into a social case, undeniably one of the more interesting.

Classical philology and linguistics flourished along with archaeology for a period before and after World War I. The young Einar Löfstedt came into contact with the study of antiquity in Imperial Germany. During his studies in Berlin and Göttingen he made the acquaintance of Wilamowitz, Norden, and Leo, the leading authorities in the field. The professorship to which he was appointed in Lund still had the old designation 'Roman oratory and poetry'. The title was in fact appropriate for one of Löfstedt's talents; he developed his rhetorical skill both as a lecturer — one term with the topic of Cicero as an orator — and later as university rector.

He succeeded to the chair occupied by the eccentric Carl Magnus Zander, a Latin scholar of the old tribe, who composed all his scholarly works, among them a book on the rhythm of Latin prose, in Latin. Löfstedt himself wrote everything from his doctor's dissertation onwards in German. In this first work he had already entered the field which was to be his own area of research, the late Latin language. Over the years he amassed an almost unique knowledge of Latin writings from a period of over five hundred years. His interest was chiefly directed towards problems of historical syntax, stylistics, and semantics. The opus which brought him European fame is entitled *Syntactica: Studien und Beiträge zur historischen Syntax des Lateins*; each page bears the stamp of his sharp powers of observation and his historical vision. In a series of longitudinal sections he presents a picture of the life and development of the Latin language from the earliest times to the Middle Ages and the emergence of the Romance languages. Löfstedt has been called Sweden's greatest Latinist ever.

Albert Wifstrand was a part of the same scholarly tradition as Löfstedt and Martin Nilsson in Sweden and Wilamowitz-Moellendorff and Gilbert Murray in Europe. After his doctoral dissertation on the Greek epigram, he devoted himself to the study of imperial hexameter poetry, its metre and style. Another of his fields was late Greek prose; he published eight slim volumes of his interpretations and emendations of Greek prose writers from imperial times. He was phenomenally well read in various periods of Greek literature, but his early death meant that the great work on the stylistic history of Greek prose which he was working on was never completed.

Wifstrand was at once a philologist and a historian of ideas; he was captivated by the encounter of the classical and the biblical. Beyond all idealized visions of a 'Pseudo-Greece' — the image of neo-classicism and the 'third humanism' — he created his own, more detached picture. His orientation in modern literature enabled him to write wide-ranging essays in which he followed the wandering of literary motifs and changes of style through the millennia. In the time of specialization to which he belonged, Wifstrand was one of the few brilliant examples of a scholar with the ability to survey and synthesize a wide range of learning.

History and the social sciences. The age of source criticism

In the philosophy faculty early this century the examination regulations ensured a strong position for the subject of history. There were solid arguments for the doubling of the professorship: the influx of students, the demands of modern methods, and not least the new fields of research — economic history, the history of political ideas, social history, regional history. A second professorship duly came in 1908.

At the beginning of the century Lauritz Weibull was lecturer in history. It was he who was to give Lund its special profile in the study of history. He began his career by publishing medieval documents. During a period as acting professor in 1909 he lectured on topics from the Viking Age. He reworked these lectures and published them under the title *Kritiska undersökningar i Nordens historia omkring år 1000* ('Critical Investigations of Scandinavian History Around 1000'). The book was, in his own words, 'an attempt to apply modern historical methods to an area of Scandinavian history where this has been done in only a few cases.' He called the result in a Nietzschean formula 'a re-evaluation of hitherto established values.' While medieval history had previously relied on Snorri Sturluson and Saxo Grammaticus, Weibull dismissed everything which he considered fabulous. Out went the legendary queen Sigríðr Stórráða; the battle of Svolder was moved to the Öresund; the invincible fortress of Jomsborg with its hundred gates was relegated to the world of saga and legend. He felt from the beginning that he would be met with resistance from the entire generation of Swedish historians who had been influenced by the ideology of a national culture.

As an avowed opponent of the romantic idealistic view of history and later historical traditionalism, Weibull demanded that historians should subject their sources to a critical scrutiny, selecting the best from them, disclosing all the tendencies concealed in the evidence, and that when reconstructing a course of events they should reject all loose hypotheses and banish personal and political preferences. With his strong faith in the virtue of scientific objectivity he was scarcely conscious of the fact that not even he himself worked without preconceptions. His own view of history was conditioned by the liberal ideas of the time, and his view of the protagonists of history bore the stamp of a rigid, sometimes almost Machiavellian psychology.

He expressed his attitudes to controversial historical problems in Scandinavian and early Swedish history in a great number of investigations. There were violent disputes about his person, his method, and his results before he finally, at the age of 49, got his chair. At the faculty meetings where the appointment was debated, the sympathies for the various candidates had partly been divided along lines of politics or cultural policy. Weibull's accession to the chair in 1919 has been linked to the democratic parliamentary reform two years previously; a new age required, or was prepared to accept, a new, critical, and less nationalistic view of the past.

His vision of history and his critical principles were to colour the journal *Scandia* which was started in 1927, with himself as editor. At his side he had a sympathizer and comrade-in-arms in his brother Curt Weibull, who soon afterwards became professor of history in Gothenburg. Within a few decades most professors of history in Sweden were Weibullians.

Stimuli from a number of scholars were absorbed by Lauritz Weibull and blended in his own highly distinctive, obstinate personality. He combined his ascetic and purist methodology with an analysis of texts and legends which revealed aesthetic discernment. Yet this critic of tradition was — one of the contradictions in his nature — at the same time zealous in the preservation of local traditions, both Scandinavian and Lundensian. For a long period he was chairman of the Academic Union. At the feast to welcome the newly enrolled students on the fourth of October, he greeted the novices in a grandiose style; he displayed the same magnificence in his capacity of alderman of the Guild of Canute in Lund. At the licentiate seminars in history, which often repaired to his home, he was an uncrowned chieftain, who conducted the conversation with elegance and with caustic arrogance towards those who dissented from his views. 'The Weibullians became a sect,' one of the participants wrote, 'if not exactly for mutual admiration, then at least for mutual stimulation and — competition. Lund was the centre of the world, and most Lundensian of all was the Weibullian school.' The unbelievers outside this school felt that Weibull often carried his source criticism to the point of hypercriticism. Moreover, he undeniably took pleasure in adopting paradoxical stances; on every point he wished to say something different from what his predecessors had said.

In this respect as in many others, the other professor of history in Lund, Gottfrid Carlsson, was his opposite. Gottfrid Carlsson was a conservative historian. Like Weibull, his period was the Middle Ages, and his method involved a critical examination of the sources, but with greater reserve than his colleague; as a contrast and a complement to Weibull he exerted considerable influence and also acquired a large circle of disciples.

The differences between the two were sharpened in the darkening political and ideological climate of the 1930s and 1940s. With his early orientation towards France, it was natural that Lauritz Weibull, a supporter of the *entente cordiale* during the First World War, should remain in the liberal, anti-Nazi camp. He was profoundly shocked by the disaster which befell Denmark when it was invaded and contact with Copenhagen severed. His best friends and sympathizers belonged to the Danish school of source criticism which numbered Kristian Erslev and Erik Arup among its members.

The lines drawn up by Lauritz Weibull for historical research were maintained by his disciples; his immediate successor, Sture Bolin, demonstrated this in the precise critical method he applied to archaeological and numismatic evidence in his doctoral dissertation on Roman coin finds on Germanic soil. It was also evident in Bolin's theoretical analyses of coinage in the Roman Empire, presented in his *State and Currency in the Roman Empire* in 1958.

Ingvar Andersson, lecturer in history under Weibull and later Director General of the National Archives, likewise showed the influence of his master's methodological demands, right from his doctor's dissertation of 1928, *Källstudier till Sveriges medeltida historia* ('Studies of Sources in Medieval Swedish History'). The similarity is evident in the very choice of topic in the two volumes which Ingvar Andersson wrote on the medieval history of Scania, in which he treated his native province as the medieval centre of Scandinavia, the link between Denmark, the rest of Scandinavia, and Europe. His studies of the Nordic and European Renaissance took him to Elizabethan England and the sixteenth-century Danish features in Shakespeare's *Hamlet*. For a general public at home and also in Europe he wrote a widely read popular *History of Sweden* (1956).

One of the historical disciplines which has long had a given place at the university is Scandinavian archaeology. The subject obtained its own chair in 1919, the first professor being Otto Rydbeck. Much of his research was concentrated on the early history of Lund Cathedral; he also wrote about medieval church painting in Southern Sweden.

It was during his time that the prehistoric archaeological material was given a place beside the medieval collections in the university's Historical Museum. A separate Cathedral Museum was opened in 1932. This was yet another testimony to the interest of Lundensian archaeologists in the medieval town and its ecclesiastical monuments. Excavations during the twentieth century have provided ever richer knowledge of the medieval settlement history of Lund. The subject of medieval archaeology has in fact found its focus in Lund, with a university professorship from the 1970s.

The widely disparate fields of research which were mentioned as a motivation for the doubling of the professorship of history at the beginning of the century did not in fact begin to be explored until the inter-war years and later. The perspective has been broadened to include social science, economic history (a subject which received its own lectureship in 1949, shortly afterwards transformed into a professorship), contemporary history, and international history, with the USA in the centre. The discussion on methodology has become intense, and the preconditions for research and the view of history have been debated in a way which would not have been possible for previous generations of historians who unconsciouly accepted so much as a matter of course.

In the early years of the century the subject of political science fell within the sphere of history. As an independent subject, political science acquired its first professor, Fredrik Lagerroth, lecturer in historical political science; the subject of statistics had by then received its own chair. In a much debated doctoral dissertation Lagerroth had undertaken a re-evaluation of the tarnished reputation of the Age of Freedom in Sweden; he interpreted it as the first period of parliamentarism in Swedish history, drawing parallels with the early parliamentary tradition of England.

In his view of society and the conflicts between its centres of power, Lagerroth was inspired by the German legal scholar Otto von Gierke and his ideas on the interplay of *Herrschaft* and *Genossenschaft*. Another distinguishing feature of Lagerroth's view of Swedish constitutional history is the long perspective; he saw the reform of 1809 in its traditional Swedish context, as a history of Sweden translated into legal clauses, this in contrast to previous research which had stressed the dependence of the constitution on Montesquieu's theory of the separation of powers.

Right from the nineteenth century there had been an intimate connection between the subjects of geography and history, as was seen in the very title of the new professorship of 1897: geography and history. Geography did not achieve its position as an independent subject until 1916, when Helge Nelson became professor of geography. Nelson represented a type of research directed towards the natural sciences and the present day, with an economic and sociological bias; his doctoral dissertation had brought him close to geology.

At the request of the Commission on Emigration, Nelson undertook a study of emigration from Öland to the United States. This led to a huge geographical inventory of Swedish population groups in contemporary America; his four trips across the Atlantic to collect material and his twenty years of study were summarized in his book *The Swedes and the Swedish Settlements in North America*. He investigated such topics as the connection between the places of origin of the Swedish settlers and their choice of where to settle in the new world, taking into account factors like landscape type, environment, and climate. He studied the relations of the immigrants to other ethnic groups and their eventual assimilation. The work was of importance for the author Vilhelm Moberg, who chronicled the history of Swedish emigration in his series of novels about *The Emigrants*.

The group of subjects which include geography and political science has been affected by the changed times of the 1960s and later. A sign of the changes is the move of both subjects from the philosophy faculty to the faculty of social sciences, established in 1964.

The transformation meant that the methodology of political science, previously indebted to law and history, became clearly sociological. At the same time the interest was directed away from constitutional events of the past — such as the reform of 1809 — towards present-day constitutional development, the growth of the political parties and interest groups and their role in modern society, towards political institutions and systems, towards local and regional politics, international politics, and — in particular — political theory.

Geography underwent a process of differentiation. The subject was divided between the study of nature and culture; *naturgeografi* 'physical geography' was given a place among the natural sciences, while *kulturgeografi* 'human geography' and the new subject of economic geography joined the social sciences. The human geographers shifted their attention more towards phenomena which lend themselves to measurement and presentation in exact figures. This is one expression of the demand for quantification which permeates all the social sciences and which has partially influenced the humanities. In later years human geography has been dominated by the study of innovation and diffusion. New concepts in human geography — centre of innovation, cultural diffusion, cultural boundary, culture area — have also become important in ethnology, dialectology, and archaeology. The formation of theories and theoretical problems have generally been given a more central position than formerly.

Of Lund's human geographers the most internationally acknowledged is Torsten Hägerstrand. In his early work he concentrated on the process of diffusion. Later on he and his associates at the University of Lund developed an approach called *time geography*. The key concepts are time and space, or rather the single basic concept of time-space, together with the concepts of trajectory and station (which includes, for example, home and workplace). Using these conceptual tools, time geography analyses the time-space patterns and processes which result when individuals are seen to draw upon space and time as resources essential to the realization of particular projects. Within the framework of a lingua franca and with the frequent aid of graphical models, time geography studies the contents of human existence in time and space. The method has a high degree of abstraction and is consequently applicable in large areas of the humanities and social sciences.

Aesthetics and psychology

An academic who attained an early position of prominence in the Stockholm press was Fredrik Böök. His contributions to the 'Strindberg feud' in the 1910s had attracted great attention thanks to his stylistic talent and his polemical vigour. At the age of 24 he acquired his doctor's degree with a thesis of solid but traditional character on the subject of the early Swedish prose novel. His real breakthrough as an original scholar came in the autumn term of 1912, when his series of lectures on the analysis of literature attracted considerable attention. He published them under the title *Svenska studier i litteraturvetenskap* ('Swedish Studies in Literature'). In the lectures and the book Fredrik Böök advocated a new way of approaching literary texts, which involved an act of intellectual sympathy designed to let the reader penetrate 'the works themselves', into their 'living core', into 'the structure of the poetic organism'. This meant a break with an earlier scholarly tradition, a change of scientific outlook. Böök's lectures and his book attacked the one-sided historical approach of Henrik Schück and his school, which risked stopping outside the literary works without reaching inside them. At the same time it was a critique of a type of historical comparativism and association psychology which had adopted a mechanistic, atomistic perspective on the process of creation and the literary text.

Böök's new approach was influenced by French and German philosophers and scholars who had broken with the positivistic ideal which had hitherto dominated science. In Germany around the turn of the century there was a lively debate concerning the relation between the natural sciences and the cultural disciplines. Philosophers like Wilhelm Dilthey and Heinrich Rickert challenged the claim that the study of culture could be subjected to the generalized concepts of the natural scientists; they asserted instead that the natural sciences sought general laws, while the humanities sought the individual, the unique, *das Einmalige*. The duty of the natural scientist was to 'explain', while that of the humanist was to 'understand', to arrive at a profound interpretation of an individual event or an individual text.

Böök urged that literature should be interpreted on the basis of total empathy. He advocated the *Einfühlung* of the aesthetician Theodor Lipps and the *intuition* of the French philosopher Bergson. Böök had in fact heard Bergson lecture while in Paris on a travel scholarship. While there he also attended seminars held by the leading literary historian of the age, Gustave Lanson, whose concrete *explications de texte* he admired, but whose one-sided historical outlook was at that time an object of controversy at the Sorbonne. All these stimuli were blended in the series of lectures which became Böök's *Svenska studier i litteraturvetenskap*. Böök put the ideas of his new programme into practice in a series of model analyses of Swedish poetry ranging in time from the Romantic Age down to contemporary poets.

Two fields of research dominated Böök's later work: Romanticism and the close of the nineteenth century. He made lasting contributions to the study of Tegnér (a pet topic of Lundensian scholars). Concrete tasks involving the editing of texts and the writing of literary biographies led him back to historical and comparative methods, which he renewed and developed.

He lectured on the subject of the Romantic Age. He wrote a comprehensive survey of the period for a joint work on the history of literature, in which he was also responsible for the section on literary development in Sweden during the 1880s and 1890s.

For more than a decade he worked with enormous energy and concentration. He attained the goal of his academic career in 1920, when he became professor of the now independent subject of the history of literature and poetics; shortly before this, the history of art had been given its own chair. He left this position after a few years, however, to write for the Stockholm press. For his journalistic writings he created an essayistic form which allowed him to treat widely varying topics, whether literary, historical, biographical, or political. During the First World War he had been strongly committed to the side of Germany; he was closely associated with the '1914 ideas', as they were known. In the 1930s he was seduced by the new ideas coming from Hitler's Germany.

When he returned to scholarship after his political débâcle he devoted his last years to the writing of a wide-ranging number of works of biography and literary history. Like his acknowledged master Sainte-Beuve and his unacknowledged master in the genre, Georg Brandes, he applied in these works a psychological-biographical method: works of literature were interpreted as reflections of experiences and conflicts in the writers' lives. Böök's later biographical books include not only studies of various Swedish authors but also an outstanding work on Hans Christian Andersen, which appeared in Danish, Dutch, and in an English translation published in the USA in 1962. He also wrote some parts of a history of European literature which was long used as a textbook at the university, as was his survey of Swedish literature.

Despite — or perhaps by virtue of — his subjectivity, despite his tendency to allow pet notions to distort his view of the literary works under consideration, Fredrik Böök's scholarship represents one of the most impressive contributions to the humanities in Lund University in the twentieth century.

Fredrik Böök's audacious and exuberant disposition, his expansive, dynamic, and often unpredictable temperament made him a sharp contrast to the student friend and eating companion of his early years, Albert Nilsson. Yet they shared a profound interest and enthusiasm for romantic philosophy and literature. Both applied themselves to questions of aesthetics, psychology, and the history of ideas; both were influenced by the new trends in the study of literature which were characteristic of contemporary German research into Romanticism.

Albert Nilsson, who had the greater philosophical talent of the two, was the Swedish pioneer of the study of literature in the context of the history of ideas. He had spent a term at the University of Berlin, where he heard Friedrich Paulsen lecture on Schopenhauer. Like all those of his contemporaries who were interested in philosophy, he was impressed by Friedrich Albert Lange's *Geschichte des Materialismus*, a work in the neo-Kantian spirit.

In 1916 Albert Nilsson published a literary history of Swedish idealism, entitled *Svensk romantik: Den platonska strömningen* ('Swedish Romanticism: The Platonic Current'). In this work, based on his lectures, he follows the ideas of Plato, the Neoplatonists, and Schelling as they appear in the Swedish romantic poets. It was in this work that he applied to the study of literature in Sweden a method of interpretation based on the history of ideas; at the same time he laid the foundations for later generations of students of Romanticism.

The tradition of literary scholarship in Lund was continued by Fredrik Böök's and Albert Nilsson's pupils. Aesthetic, psychological, and general philosophical problems characterize the highly original work published in the 1920s by one of these, Olle Holmberg; the title is *Inbillningens värld* ('The World of Imagination'). Borrowing elements from many sources, from Kantian philosophy, from German *Kulturpsychologie*, from Nietzsche, Freud, and Kretschmer, from Croce's theory of art and Bergson's philosophy, Olle Holmberg created his own aesthetics.

153

Holmberg's interest was concentrated on individual authors, whom he studied for their psychology and for the way they reflected the ideas and history of their times. As regards both literature and personality he was closely associated with the Lund authors of his own generation, of whom he produced intimate literary portraits. He was the first professor of the history of literature in Sweden to include contemporary literature in undergraduate courses; he was well acquainted with modern literature through his work as a critic for the newspaper *Dagens Nyheter*.

His sensitivity, inventiveness, and quick wit are also evident in his essays and aphorisms; he developed the essay into a personal art form. As a lecturer in the history of literature during the 1920s and 1930s he displayed a basically ironic distance, a talent for understatement, and a detached style which made him a typical representative of 'Lund scepticism', as it was called. Yet in the face of the power of darkness that was Nazism he revealed himself as an uncomprising resistance fighter. In his writings and his actions he waged an indefatigable struggle against the fellow-travellers of fascism both inside and outside the university; he organized aid for Scandinavian academics and authors in German prisons and concentration camps. It was also on his personal initiative that a representative of 'the other Germany', Thomas Mann — the contemporary writer whom he probably esteemed most highly — was awarded an honorary doctorate at Lund University after the end of World War II.

The growing number of students on all levels, from undergraduate to doctoral, justified the doubling of the professorship of literature in the 1940s. In 1970 the scope of the subject was the reason adduced for the addition of a third chair, with the designation literature, particularly drama.

The first occupant of the second chair of literary history and poetics created in 1948 was Algot Werin. Like Hans Larsson in an earlier generation, he displayed a harmonious blend of the agrarian heritage and the urban academic tradition. He was the foremost Tegnér scholar of his generation. Much of his work shows the depths of his regional roots, yet with a European outlook towards the heritage of Goethe and Nietzsche. His work is a part of the tradition of Swedish idealism and the Swedish nineteenth century, about which he published two collections of essays.

New viewpoints and new methods in the field of comparative literature have been developed, partly through the interplay with students of sociology and communication. The subject has been transformed; once concentrated around biography, psychology, and the history of ideas, it has now become dominated by the concepts first of *œuvre*, then of *text*. As with other arts subjects, what has been won in terms of terminological and methodological stringency has at times risked a loss of general accessibility and cultural importance.

Thomas Mann, who had been stripped of his honorary doctorate from Bonn during Hitler's time, received an honorary doctorate in Lund in the spring of 1949. Here he is in the procession to the cathedral, escorted by his two 'marshals'.

The history and theory of art, as the newly independent subject was called in the 1920s, had its foremost representative in Ragnar Josephson, who was appointed professor in 1929. One of his early teachers in the subject at Uppsala acquainted him with Heinrich Wölfflin's theory of the 'intuitive forms' of art, which directed much of Josephson's research and teaching.

His inaugural lecture was on the subject of the Roman spirit in Swedish art, a theme which retained its importance throughout his career. As a teacher it was his ambition to confront his students in various ways with the creative art of the present day. He gave them a schooling in modern exhibition techniques by having them serve at the Scanian Art Museum associated with his department. He himself was in intimate contact with contemporary painters and sculptors. In their studios he observed the process which led from trial pieces and sketches to completed works; at his seminars he often brought up the topic of the birth of works of art, with reference to concrete material.

This was to form the basis of his synoptic book *Konstverkets födelse* ('The Birth of a Work of Art'), which appeared in the ominous year 1940. He had elaborated a method of form analysis which enabled him to follow the stages in the creative artistic process. He borrowed the idea of evolution from the natural sciences and applied it to the field of the human spirit. Yet positivistic, deterministic philosophy is defeated; into the system he has built Bergson's ideas about the progress of the creative process by leaps. A final result of Josephson's studies was the Art Museum which he built up; the museum houses preliminary sketches and plaster casts of monumental art from Sweden and the rest of Scandinavia and Europe, in particular France.

He was captivated by the artistic act, perceived as a feat of heroism, and by the personality of the genius. He himself was not unconversant with theatrical gestures. For a few years he took a leave of absence from his professorship, his interest in drama and his commitment to the theatre having led him to the position of director of the Dramatic Theatre in Stockholm. He returned to Lund and continued his work in research, museums, and lecturing. He was one of the classically histrionic lecturers, his powerful rhetoric and his mighty vocal resources spellbinding a full auditorium. His last residence in Lund was the house where Strindberg had stayed during his alchemical period in the 1890s.

For a decade the aesthetes and historians of literature and art had a distinguished guest in their midst in the person of Hans Ruin, who had a scholarship as Nordic lector, and later a position as research fellow. He came from Helsinki, where Yrjö Hirn was his teacher in aesthetics. Early travels in Europe in the inter-war years, in the Germany of the expressionists and Ludwig Klages, in the France of Bergson and Abbé Brémond, shaped his personality as a European intellectual and an astute culture critic. In Finland he had links with the young generation of authors; during the Finnish-Soviet 'Winter War' of 1939–1940 and its continuation, he was the official cultural representative of his country, liaising with the foreign press and making frequent lecture trips to Sweden.

When he came to Lund in the mid-1940s his lectures were among the best attended. The artistically constructed lectures became a series of books in the frontier zone between literary psychology and art psychology. He published a study of twentieth-century art based on *Gestalt* psychology; entitled 'La psychologie structurale et l'art moderne', it appeared in the 1949 number of the international philosophical periodical *Theoria*, which was at that time published in Lund. He was a final link in the chain of Lundensian aesthetics, the scholarly tradition of Hans Larsson, Albert Nilsson, Ragnar Josephson, and Olle Holmberg. Hans Ruin's major work, *Poesiens mystik* ('The Mystique of Poetry'), although from an earlier phase in his career, experienced a revival when he published a revised edition during his years in Lund; he brought both the literary and the scientific aspects up to date. With his aesthetic sensitivity and his pose as a solo artist, he was one of the last of the cavaliers of Beauty.

The work of John Landquist belongs to an area which overlaps literature, aesthetics, philosophy, psychology, and education. He had studied in Uppsala, but there was no place for him in a university dominated by the heritage of Boström and Hägerström. In his youth he had gone to Paris to hear Henri Bergson, whose work he helped to introduce to Sweden; in Vienna he had visited Sigmund Freud, whose book on *The Interpretation of Dreams* he translated into Swedish. In 1920 he published in Freud's journal *Imago* an article which was later to be famous: 'Das künstlerische Symbol'; in it he points out the similarity between the way an artist creates a picture and the condensation mechanism in dreams. Landquist also earlier introduced Heinrich Rickert's philosophy of history and Wilhelm Dilthey's hermeneutics.

He issued his inaugural lecture as professor of education and psychology as a slim volume which soon became a textbook in his subject. The book is called *Själens enhet* ('The Unity of the Mind'), a manifesto directed against the outmoded association psychology. His ideas about the holistic aspirations of all conscious life are connected to German *Gestalt* psychology. In the book he examines the difference between three main forms of psychological research: experimental, medical, and humanistic. He himself represented humanistic psychology.

Of his pupils during the ten years when he was professor in Lund, no less that eight later became professors in the two subjects which his chair comprised, psychology and education. His professorship was later divided among three successors, resulting in a chair of psychology, one of pedagogy and educational psychology (both of which were later moved to the faculty of social sciences), and a third in practical education, located at the Malmö School of Education.

Since Landquist's time the trend in psychology in Lund has been towards mainly dynamic, experimental research into personality. Perception psychology has come into the foreground. Ingenious techniques, such as rapid exposure to neutral or menacing pictures, have been developed to assist the study and interpretation of pre-conscious stages of perception. Methods which illustrate the experiment subjects' perception of reality and their defence mechanisms have found wide clinical application. Psychological and psychiatric research have gone hand in hand and are welcomed as a bridge built between two subjects and two faculties.

Without repudiating the gains made by experimental and medical psychology, the retiring professor of psychology — Gudmund Smith — in his farewell lecture in 1986 once again formulated the demand and need for humanistic psychology. What is required, he noted, is 'a drive for the genuine understanding of Man, not for the technically advanced but contentually anaemic variety which has characterized the subject at many of the world's universities for decades.'

Still among the aesthetic disciplines, it has only been for shorter periods that the history of music has been regularly represented at the university. The first lecturer in the subject was Tobias Norlind, whose lectureship had the original combination of the history of literature and music, between 1909 and 1919.

Tobias Norlind's course syllabus for the history and theory of music for 1914 still survives. It includes works of Swedish and German musical scholarship, books by Riemann and Kretzschmar, as well as by himself; the first scientific attempts at a history of Swedish music were written by Norlind. He had studied music abroad, in Leipzig and Munich. At the end of his career he was teaching the history of music and aesthetics at the conservatory in Stockholm, where he had the title of professor. A regular chair of musicology was created and filled in 1986.

A humanistic credo

During the final year of the First World War, before the November 1918 armistice, the celebration of the university's bicentennial did not receive any great attention. Of the guests from war-torn Europe, only one made a speech: a representative of the country, Germany, and the town, Greifswald, with which Lund University had had the longest and closest contacts over the years. The celebrations were given a markedly Nordic character owing to the presence of representatives from Denmark, Norway, and Finland. At the commemoration in the cathedral the main speech was held by the rector of the university and its chief orator, Johan C. W. Thyrén. He had chosen to shed light on a question which had confounded Rousseau and which the war had once again raised: 'What is the relation between scientific progress and the progress of humanity?' The speech concluded on a disquieting note; he warned that the verdict passed on the time would be 'too much technique and too little culture.'

Hopeful of the triumph of the humanities and of humanism in the Europe of the future, the Royal Society of the Humanities was founded in conjunction with the university bicentennial. Since the eighteenth century the Physiographic Society had provided an association for scholars in medicine and the natural sciences. The advance of the humanistic disciplines in the nineteenth century and the early twentieth naturally led to creation of a comparable society for the arts subjects.

The purpose of the new society was twofold: partly to stimulate the publication of academic works in a series of Acta, and partly to resume scholarly contacts with Europe on the reopening of the frontiers after the end of the war. In 1920 Ulrich von Wilamowitz-Moellendorff came from Berlin to lecture on 'Hellenentum und Antike'. From the same city came Adolf von Harnack and Hermann Diels, both theological scholars. From the University of Berlin came the art historian Wilhelm Pinder, from Paris the linguist Antoine Meillet, from Rome the historian of religion Franz Cumont, from Basel the Germanist Andreas Heusler, from Munich the medievalist Paul Lehmann. Since the end of World War II the society has been visited by scholars like Jean Festugière, the historian of religion from Paris, Kemp Malone, the Baltimore philologist, Thomas Mann from his new home in Zurich, and Louis Hjelmslev, the structural linguist from Copenhagen.

The year 1920 saw the founding of a complementary, at first competitive, sister organization, the New Society of Letters in Lund. The purpose was to provide a meeting-place and a publication series chiefly for younger, 'unpromoted' scholars. The constitution stipulated that no one over the age of 55 might be co-opted as an ordinary member; this guaranteed a constant rejuvenation of the society. The work of the New Society of Letters has also helped to encourage research in the humanities and contacts both inside and outside the scholarly community.

Science and technology in the twentieth century

In the nineteenth century Lund was renowned primarily as a centre for the study of the humanities. Science and medicine have come to the fore during the twentieth century; in terms of the amount of research and the number of students, these disciplines began to dominate after World War II. This is the effect of a scientific revolution which is greater in scale than perhaps any hitherto in history. It has meant radical changes in fundamental concepts and methods, and it has led to a society where atomic fission, DNA technology, lasers, and computers have transformed our world.

The following pages attempt only a few fragmentary pictures of the history of Lundensian science and mathematics in the twentieth century.

The position of pure mathematics had been weak in the nineteenth century. Seminars in mathematics became a regular feature of university teaching in 1874, when Emanuel Björling was appointed professor. His special fields were solid geometry and plane geometry; his textbook in the latter subject, published in 1890, was used in geometry teaching throughout Scandinavia up to the 1920s.

In Björling's time the extraordinary professor of mechanics and mathematical physics was Victor Bäcklund, whose achievements as a scholar were more significant. The results he obtained on the theory of partial differential equations have been called the greatest contribution to mathematics in Sweden for the time; a special class of transformations have been called after him, 'Bäcklund transformations'.

Since then, mathematics in Lund has witnessed a number of remarkable vicissitudes and achievements. One of the young lecturers, Anders Wiman, was initially trained in the geometrical school. A Danish mathematician, Niels Erik Nørlund, became professor at the age of 27. There had not been a Danish professor in Lund since the first decades of the university; now after an interval of two centuries, two Danes were appointed to chairs in quick succession: first Nørlund and then the historian of religion Edvard Lehmann. Nørlund's specialist fields were differential equations and special functions. He was for a long time editor of Acta Mathematica. After a decade in Lund he returned to Copenhagen in 1922 to become professor of mathematics.

In the next generation Lund had two outstanding mathematicians in Nils Zeilon and Marcel Riesz. The former worked with partial differential equations; one of his achievements was the solution of a problem which had been posed by the Italian mathematical physicist Volterra, which involved a complete analysis of double refraction in a crystal.

Marcel Riesz was Hungarian by birth, the younger brother of the even more celebrated mathematician Fredric Riesz. He had come to Sweden in 1910 on a scholarship from the Mittag-Leffler Institute in Stockholm. He was a specialist in the theory of series and related problems, but he later broadened his interests to cover a wide area. Along with one of the most prominent mathematicians of the twentieth century, G.F. Hardy in Cambridge, he published a famous book in 1915, *The General Theory of Dirichlet's Series*.

Riesz was a mathematician of the continental type, with many contacts in Europe and the USA. After his retirement he spent ten years as a research professor in the United States. As a gentleman of unique learning he lived above all for and through his scholarship, a stimulating teacher for advanced students. Two of them who became professors in the next generation were Gårding and Hörmander. They have expressed their gratitude for what they learnt from the dynamic genius Riesz, not least through listening to his oral communications, expressed in broken Swedish as he walked through the peaceful streets of Lund, gesticulating lavishly. Marcel Riesz is one of several examples of the stimulus which Lund — the small-town university with the risk of academic inbreeding and stagnation — has received from scholars of foreign blood and origin.

The next revolution in mathematics which was around the corner had more to do with technical development than mathematical theory. The first electronic computer in Lund was completed in 1956. There had previously been only one in the country, known by the acronym BESK, which also means 'bitter'. Its counterpart in Lund was christened SMIL 'smile', a more appropriate name for the Lund temperament; it had 2000 electronic valves and a capacity of 10,000 operations per minute, but it is long since a thing of the past. A post of demonstrator in numerical analysis was created, raised to a professorship in 1965. The new age of information theory and information technology had arrived. Computers made their entry across the board.

In astronomy Charlier was succeeded in 1929 by Knut Lundmark. His research concerned the nature of foreign galaxies and their cosmological position. While still only a student at Uppsala he undertook a study trip to the Mount Wilson Observatory in the USA. One method which he used to determine distances in space was the observation of novae; the eleven novae in the Andromeda galaxy were of special interest to astronomers at this time. Lundmark's studies of the phenomenon led him to investigations into the history of astronomy, including Tycho Brahe's corresponding observations. He launched the hypothesis that the star which led the three wise men to the manger in Bethlehem was a nova. Evidence of his international recognition is the fact that a page is devoted to him in Taton's *Histoire générale des sciences*, together with the naming of a newly discovered planet — admittedly a small planet — after him, Lundmarka.

A couple of centuries had passed since Spole used his primitive telescope to make the first astronomical observations of the horizon in Lund. In Lundmark's time the observatory in Gyllenkroks Allé felt the need for larger and more modern instruments, especially a bigger reflector. A wish was also expressed for a subsidiary observatory on a site which would be more suitable for observations. The result was the opening in 1965 of the new observatory with a modern reflecting telescope at Jävan on the ridge of Romeleåsen. Lundmark was dead and gone by then; a new generation of astronomers were waiting to carry on his work. Air pollution and light conditions soon forced astronomers away from Scania. Lund's astronomers now carry on their observations on other latitudes. In 1986 work was begun on the construction of an ultra-modern telescope for use at the observatory in La Palma in the Canary Islands. Modern technology enables astronomers to study galaxies which originated twelve to fifteen million years ago, soon after the first big bang. The research project is a joint Scandinavian venture; astronomers in Lund have the equipment and the technology necessary to control and receive pictures from the telescope in La Palma.

A historian of Uppsala University remarked that 'in physics, the light came from Lund'; he was referring to two expatriate Lundensians who were professors of physics in the sister university, Wilhelm Oseen and Manne Siegbahn. Oseen was originally a mathematician who became a pioneer in the field of mathematical physics. His particular speciality was hydrodynamics. He corrected the theory of wave movement in currents and stated a method for calculating resistance to the movement of a body in water. In 1909 he became professor of mechanics and mathematical physics in Uppsala.

Manne Siegbahn was a lecturer in physics under Janne Rydberg, for whom he deputized and then succeeded as professor in 1920. Most of his work was in X-ray spectroscopy, in particular that part which deals with the measurement of wavelengths in X-ray spectra. His new designs for X-ray tubes and air pumps allowed for an increase in the intensity of radiation used in experiments. The spectrographs which he invented for various wavelengths also ensured greater accuracy than previous measurements. This was significant for the explanation of the periodic system which the Danish atomic physicist Niels Bohr was developing at this time.

In 1924 Siegbahn succeeded in demonstrating optical refraction in X-rays; his discoveries brought him a Nobel Prize in physics. By that time he had left the department in Lund, which many researchers from Sweden and abroad had visited. He was invited to fill the corresponding chair in Uppsala. After receiving a personal chair in the Academy of Sciences and taking over the direction of its physics research department, he built up one of Sweden's most modern institutes for research in atomic physics.

The little department in Lund which he left in the twenties was cramped for space. Plans for a new building were delayed by the Second World War, and it was not until 1950 that a new building was completed. The new department was given considerable material and human resources. New fields of specialization were added at a rapid pace, among them atomic spectroscopy with Bengt Edlén. His spectroscopic studies mostly concerned the spectra of highly ionized atoms. His systematic comparative investigations made it possible to analyse complex spectra and to correct and extend earlier analyses. In 1941 he succeeded in interpreting a number of previously unexplained lines in the spectrum of the solar corona. He was able to show that they came from iron, nickel, calcium, and other elements in a state of high ionization. The discovery was important for astrophysics, since it proved that the temperature of the solar corona was considerably higher than had previously been assumed.

Other physicists of international rank from Lund include Gunnar Källén and Sven Gösta Nilsson. Both died young after significant early accomplishments.

Gunar Källén's early interest in quantum electrodynamic phenomena led to his participation in the development of quantum theory. On the recommendation of Niels Bohr, Robert Oppenheimer, and Wolfgang Pauli, a personal chair of theoretical physics was created for him at Lund in 1958. In the 1960s his interest was focused on elementary particle physics. A series of lectures on this became the core of his book published in 1964, *Elementary Particles*, a work of interest to theoreticians and experimentalists alike.

Sven Gösta Nilsson held the professorship of mathematical physics. Like the other Lund physicists he was in close contact with scientists at the Bohr Institute in Copenhagen; he was for several years visiting professor at the University of California in Berkeley. He made precise mathematical calculations in order to chart the field of force inside the nucleus of the atom; his calculations were later verified by experiment. It has been said of him that he knew every nucleus personally. His name is primarily associated with the independent particle model, also called after him the Nilsson model. He went on to study current problems in nuclear physics, including pair production and superheavy nuclei.

One of the great scientific projects of the eighties is known as Project MAX, an acronym for Microtron Accelerator for X-rays. The third-generation accelerator in Lund has pushed the research front forwards not only in physics but also in chemistry, medicine, and biology; up to six experiments with synchrotron light can be run in parallel.

Contacts between physicists in Lund and Copenhagen have been vigorous ever since Niels Bohr, acclaimed for his work on atomic structures, became professor and director of the Copenhagen Institute of Theoretical Physics. After the Second World War had ended, Copenhagen's position as the centre of Scandinavian research in theoretical physics was given official recognition with the founding of the organization called Nordita. It was formed with financial support from all the Nordic countries; Niels Bohr played a major role in the planning of the organization, as did his close friend and colleague in Lund, Torsten Gustafson, professor of mechanics and mathematical physics.

A leading principle for development in the natural sciences has long been segmentation into specialist areas. In chemistry, for example, the professorship was first divided into chairs of inorganic chemistry and physical chemistry, with the later addition of chairs of organic chemistry, thermochemistry, and biochemistry. Since the 1960s, however, Lund has seen the growth of a tendency which is in part intended to counteract the effects of this differentiation. A Chemistry Centre was founded with the aim of co-ordinating research and the application of its results. This was the first such scientific centre in Lund. Later examples have come in the mid-eighties: a bioscience centre and a centre for food technology are both under construction at the time of writing, and a decision was taken in 1986 to create an interdisciplinary economics centre.

The growth of institutes of this type is in a more profound sense typical of a tendency in modern scientific research. Chemistry, physics, and biology have in fact always extended beyond their traditional boundaries. Much of the work which may be of great significance for the future is being carried on within the shifting, undogmatic framework of new intermediate areas with names like microbiology, molecular biology, and biochemistry. Lund found an original representative of the synthetic genius of modern times in the figure of Gösta Ehrensvärd, from 1956 the first professor of biochemistry.

Far back, in what now seem like prehistoric times, all the science subjects could be housed in a single building, and even further back they were under a single professor. But a spiralling development and a new holistic view of physical, chemical, and biological processes have nevertheless in a sense brought us back to a time when all the various subjects are part of a single concept.

The period from 1914 to 1930 was a time of fruitful expansion for the study of minerals and rocks. A department of mineralogy and petrography grew up in Lund. The physicist Manne Siegbahn was commissioned by the department to construct an X-ray tube designed to suit the requirements of geologists. It was later to be known as 'the Hadding tube'.

It was with the aid of this that Assar Hadding, who started his work at the department in the second decade of this century, carried on his crystallographical research. Familiar with petrographical methods from his years studying in Heidelberg under one of the leading geological authorities of the time, E.A. Wülfing, Hadding came to an early realization of the potential value of X-rays in the analysis of crystals. Apart from his work in this field, he is known for his investigations into that part of petrography which concerns itself with sedimentary rocks.

As a consequence of the general expansion of the natural sciences, the professorship of geology was doubled shortly after the end of the Second World War; there was now a professor specializing in petrography and mineralogy, and one specializing in historical geology. There was a further differentiation within the subject in 1962.

In zoology, David Bergendahl's successor was Hans Wallengren. He did his research in protozoa, primitive single-cell animals. He was also the first in Sweden to introduce physiology as a part of zoology; he himself taught courses in zoophysiology and the histology of vertebrate animals.

It was under Wallengren's leadership that the department of zoology was given a new building, completed during the First World War. For the first time there was room for a pedagogical display of the extensive collections which had been amassed over the centuries — not just Retzius' and Sven Nilsson's finds of the skeletons and bones of aurochs and bison.

In Wallengren's time a second professorship of zoology was added. The occupants of the two chairs in the next generation were Bertil Hanström and Torsten Gislén. The former studied invertebrate anatomy and physiology, and, in line with the contemporary interest in internal secretory organs and hormone functions, he came to devote more and more of his research to the role of hormones; this included his great work *Hormones in Invertebrates*. His colleague, the versatile and inventive Torsten Gislén, pursued research in marine biology on the west coast of Sweden, his speciality being the echinoderm phylum (starfish and other spiny creatures). It was Gislén who introduced both the concept and the subject of ecology to zoology in Lund. The zoological fields of research have been segmented into three subjects, each with its own professor: structural zoology, systematic zoology, and animal physiology.

Marine biological research has been undertaken along the west coast, both at Kristineberg (north of Gothenburg) and in the Öresund.

There has also been a tendency towards differentiation in the development of biology. The pioneer of the new subject of genetics was Herman Nilsson-Ehle, who put the new knowledge to practical application in plant breeding.

Genetics as a scientific subject had been founded by Gregor Mendel in the 1860s. His work, however, had fallen into oblivion and went unnoticed until the turn of the century. It was Bengt Lidforss who introduced Mendel to Sweden, along with the originator of mutation theory, Hugo de Vries; from about 1910 the study of heredity was metamorphosed as a result of the chromosome theory.

Nilsson-Ehle's work marked the start of the time when the new insights could be confirmed in theory and put into practice. Early this century he had led the work of improving oats and wheat at the Svalöv Seed Association. Alongside the practical experiments he investigated the theoretical conditions necessary for plant improvement. He presented his results in a doctoral dissertation on cross-breeds in 1909. This book, which was followed by a long series of works, brought him to the first rank of international experts on heredity.

He developed Mendel's theory of heredity by demonstrating complicating factors which explained hitherto obscure variations in the transmission of hereditary characteristics. He investigated mutations and proved that X-rays can increase their frequency. He crossed plants which possessed valuable characteristics and succeeded in producing new varieties. These new plants from Svalöv have been of fundamental importance for the development of Swedish agriculture. They helped to make Sweden self-sufficient in 1940, when the country was cut off by war; there was thus no repeat of the crop failures and food scarcity which had affected Sweden during the First World War.

Nilsson-Ehle also worked to increase the yields in forestry and fruit-growing; he discovered a triploid giant aspen in Scania and encouraged research into tetraploid organisms and crosses. Back in the middle of the eighteenth century, when a professorship in 'natural history' was first established, the justification was the utility which agriculture and the economy could derive from a systematic study of botany. It took 150 years before the expectations were completely fulfilled.

Nilsson-Ehle's suggestive force helped to assemble many disciples who formed a school of young geneticists, several of whom continued the work of plant improvement. Genetics has since been further developed through an association with research into cells. A leading scholar in genetically oriented cytology was Arne Müntzing, professor of genetics from 1938. His doctoral dissertation on the genus *Galeopsis* in 1930 has been described as a milestone in the history of modern genetics. He was the first to succeed in producing in the laboratory a Linnaean species — *Galeopsis tetrahit*, the hemp-nettle — by increasing the chromosomes. Following in Nilsson-Ehle's footsteps, his experiments in crossing have led to new seed varieties with double or cumulative chromosome counts: rye-wheat, tetraploid rye, and barley.

Chromosome research in Lund has covered not only plant genetics but also human genetics. The foremost name here is Albert Levan. He began his work on chromosomes with studies in botany and applications in plant breeding. His most celebrated discovery, however, came in 1956, when he managed in collaboration with a Chinese scientist to establish the number and identity of the forty-six chromosomes which determine hereditary characteristics in humans. His work in cancer chromosome research has opened new horizons for both genetics and medicine.

A special area of botany where Lund has had a special position ever since the two Agardhs is the study of algae. The leading scientist in the field in the twentieth century has been Harald Kylin. Three families of red algae bear his name: Kylinia, Kyliniella, and Haraldia.

Darwin's theoretical construct, which won immediate supporters in Lund, has also in latter years met an opponent. Through an irony of history, a pupil of Bengt Lidforss, Heribert Nilsson, came to adopt a paradoxical anti-Darwinist stance. His research has been primarily into the genus *Salix*. Nilsson was an orthodox follower of Mendel, but was sceptical about Darwin. In a work on the origin of species he claimed that there had never been any continuous, progressive revolution. He assumed instead, like Cuvier at the beginning of the nineteenth century, that a series of huge catastrophes caused by extraterrestrial forces had brought about rapid changes in the plant and animal world and almost entirely eradicated the flora and fauna which had existed before.

Like so many other disciplines, botany has seen increasing specialization. Newer fields which have acquired professorships include plant ecology and limnology. The latter subject, the ecology of fresh waters, has had its own chair since 1929; research is pursued at the limnological laboratory at Aneboda.

As a counter to the differentiation within botany and zoology there has been a noticeable trend towards interdisciplinary cooperation. A new ecology centre has been created in the 1980s, where the ecological subjects — including limnology, plant ecology, and animal ecology — have been brought together into one department.

The rapid growth of industrialization in post-war Sweden and the rocketing developments in technology have led to an enormous demand for technicians and engineers with higher education. Sweden had had two colleges of technology since the nineteenth century, one in the capital Stockholm, one in the maritime and industrial city of Gothenburg. Relatively few students from the south of the country applied for admission to these colleges; this alone was argument enough for the location of a third college of technology in the Lund/Malmö area. A further advantage of this siting was the possibility of close contacts with the university's faculty of mathematics and natural sciences.

Following a university commission in the 1950s and an act of parliament, higher education for engineers was initiated in Lund in 1961. It began modestly in old premises, but an intensive phase of construction between 1962 and 1967 resulted in a range of new building complexes, the sites for which were provided by the town of Lund. The college of technology was the first in the country where several buildings were planned and erected in a single stage.

Lund College of Technology, known for short as LTH (*Lunds Tekniska Högskola*) was born at a fortunate time; both financial and human resources were available in plenty. The college was inaugurated in 1965. There were then twenty-eight professors, all of a younger generation; they included the town's first female professor. Initially the college was autonomous, but in 1969 it was incorporated into the university as a faculty of technology. The administrative forms of the joint organization have varied from time to time. As intended from the beginning, the college of technology has lived in practical symbiosis with the university's science faculty. Some departmental buildings and equipment are shared jointly. By contrast, research and in particular teaching in LTH have been more directly geared to the application of technology and practical training for future professional life.

Lund College of Technology grew more quickly than expected. In 1970 it had over 50 professors and 2,300 students. Ten years later the numbers had continued to grow; there were now 60 professors. Right from the start there has been vigorous international contact, primarily with the United States and Japan. A number of visiting American professors helped to build up the work of the college. From an early stage there has also been close co-operation with Swedish industry and commerce.

The mathematical and physical subjects in LTH and the corresponding disciplines in the university together form joint departments. As we have seen, integration in the field of chemistry has gone even further. One of the many advanced projects in the Chemistry Centre concerns the study of biological macromolecules by spectroscopic methods, a project led by the professor of physical chemistry, Sture Forsén.

Other work which has brought international recognition was carried out by Hellmuth Herz, a member of a famous family of European scholars, and himself professor of electrical measurement. He has studied, among other things, ultrasonics, and in 1977 he, along with the heart specialist Inge Edler, was awarded the Lasker Prize for the invention of the echocardiograph.

Interdisciplinary research of interest not least for the conservation of the environment has been carried out by Sven Johansson, professor of physics. He was rector of the College of Technology when it was still autonomous, following which he displayed his talent for diplomacy as rector of Lund University after the critical period at the end of the sixties, and later chairman of the Royal Academy of Sciences. He has worked on the Proton-Induced X-ray Method (PIXE), with the aid of which it is possible to identify many elements simultaneously in small concentrations and test samples.

Students and teachers at LTH have been quick to build up their own traditions. The students of the college changed the face of the town by wearing the white, tassled student cap of the high-school graduate, and they have also developed their own revue and carnival traditions.

The crisis which has affected the university in the 1970s and 1980s has not left the engineers unscathed. One source of anxiety is the recruitment of future research students in a time of intensified economic competitivity, where the state-financed university has difficulty in holding its own against the generous conditions offered by private industry and commerce.

Achievements in medicine

In medicine, as in the natural sciences, the twentieth century has been characterized by rapid development. New scientific discoveries and new therapeutic methods have brought about almost a total revolution. This has been made possible thanks to an army of researchers the world over, more than ever before; they have often worked in the area between medicine proper and the contiguous scientific disciplines.

The breakthrough in medicine in Lund came in the early decades of this century. The first two specialist researchers in a modern sense, who sought by experiment to solve physiological problems, both came from Uppsala. The first was Magnus Blix, who was rector of Lund University around the turn of the century. He had worked on the physiology of the senses and the muscles; in the 1880s he was the first to discover and localize the points on the skin which sense cold, heat, and pressure.

His successor was another Uppsala man, Torsten Thunberg. His early work was also in sensory physiology, but his most renowned results concerned the metabolism of tissues and the combustion of cells. In order to explain the chain-like breakdown of the various organic molecules in the organism, he launched in 1916 a new method, the methylene blue method, also known as the Thunberg method.

In 1926 he invented the barospirator, the first apparatus for artificial respiration which did not require the patient to make breathing movements; it was used primarily for the treatment of infantile paralysis. On Thunberg's initiative a modern diagnostic laboratory for chemical physiology was added to the hospital in Lund.

From his youth on he travelled extensively in Europe, studying and establishing links with leading scholars; his research on cellular combustion followed ideas suggested by men like Wieland in Munich. His close contacts in the field of European medicine brought him the task of contributing material about his specialist field to international textbooks and manuals. He has been characterized as one of the foremost researchers in the entire history of Lund University.

Another medical scholar of international rank was Charles Ernst Overton. As his name suggests, he was of English birth; he had received his scientific training in Switzerland. Before the turn of the century he had made himself known for his studies of the properties which make it possible for substances to penetrate living cells through the plasma membrane, the process known as osmosis. During the twentieth century he worked in the field of theoretical medicine, investigating the effects of narcotic drugs, which have the ability to pass quickly through the surface layer of cells; the result of this research is the theory which jointly bears his name, the Meyer-Overton theory.

In his new home town of Lund, Overton became more famous as an eccentric professor, known more for his absent-mindedness and his atrocious Swedish than for his pioneering work in medicine. He was restored to favour long after his death: in 1963, when the Nobel Prize in medicine was awarded to A.L. Hodgkin and A.F. Huxley, it was noted that their demonstration of how impulses were reproduced in the nerves and muscles confirmed the theories formulated by Overton more than fifty years previously.

Contemporary with Thunberg and Overton was John Forssman, professor of bacteriology, hygiene, and general pathology. His title alone is an indication that the differentiation of the various subjects in the medical faculty had still not gone very far. Forssman too was an internationally recognized scientist. After his early years of study at the Pasteur Institute in Paris, he devoted himself to immunological research in antigens and antibodies. It is from the first letter of his name that the F antigen has received its international designation.

Until the 1940s the faculty of medicine was small. Figures for 1912 show that the faculty then had twelve professors, four lecturers, and three licentiates with teaching duties; there was in addition a senior physician with the title of professor in charge of the hospital. These figures can be compared with the faculty of philosophy, where there were 17 professors and 26 lecturers.

It was not until after the Second World War that the medical faculty was expanded to the extent that its various departments and clinics in Lund and Malmö made it into a large faculty. Behind this expansion lay one man in particular, the professor of physiology in Lund, Georg Kahlson. He had received his basic scientific training in Germany and England; the chief object of his own research was histamine. While war was raging in Europe he started something of a crusade to improve the conditions for medical research in Sweden. By comparing conditions in other parts of the world he was able to demonstrate how Swedish medical science was on the point of stagnation. His initiative was the most important factor leading to an increase in resources to enable research in both science and medicine to reach an internationally acceptable level. One example is the expansion of his own department, that of physiology, which came to consist of five independent sections, including one for chromosome research and one for aeromedicine.

In 1948 close collaboration began between the university and Malmö General Hospital, where the post of senior physician is statutorily combined with a professorship. New research and teaching got under way quickly. The Malmö hospital's internal medicine department had one of the 'heaviest' clinical researchers in the region, Jan Waldenström. Macroglobulinaemia, a disease first identified and diagnosed by him, is also known as *morbus Waldenström*.

Much of the work at Malmö General Hospital has been dominated by research into blood chemistry. The names to mention here are Carl-Bertil Laurell and his colleague Ing-Marie Nilsson, whose research concerns coagulation and haemophilia. Another aspect of research in Malmö is the participation in world-wide projects on epidemiology under the auspices of the World Health Organization.

Development in the faculty of medicine at Lund University is typified by the differentiation of the various subjects of study. One example will serve to illustrate this. The professorship of theoretical medicine and forensic medicine which existed in 1868 has now been divided into chairs of pathology, pathological anatomy, bacteriology, virology, hygiene, social medicine, and forensic medicine. Increased diagnostic and therapeutic resources have led to the growth of a range of new specialities. Recent decades have seen the creation of chairs of neurology, neurochemistry, neurosurgery, radiotherapy, medical radiophysics, endocrinology, forensic psychiatry, and anaesthesiology.

Further instances of individual contributions to medical research may be mentioned. To Lund came one German scholar whose non-Aryan origin led to her ejection from Nazi Germany, namely Dora Jacobson. She collaborated with Swedish researchers in the field of neuroendocrinology, and later did outstanding work together with the Cambridge scholar G.W. Harris on the neural control of the anterior pituitary gland.

Nils-Åke Hillarp carried out experiments of fundamental importance in the department of histology, investigating signal substances. The research on prostaglandin which was initiated in the department of medical chemistry in Lund led to a Nobel Prize for professors Sune Bergström and Bengt Samuelsson, both of whom later moved to positions in Stockholm.

A trio consisting of Christer Owman, Bo Siesjö, and David Ingvar have carried out significant work on the brain. Their research has concerned the role of signal substances for cerebral metabolism. One of the most acclaimed achievements in the field of neurology was that of Lars Leksell. In 1959 he led the first brain operation using proton rays, and he was also the man behind echoencephalography, the sounding of the brain by means of echoes. Leksell's investigations of the mechanisms of muscle physiology were also of a high class.

A glance through the proceedings of the Medical Society in Lund will complement and concretize this brief summary of the recent history of medicine in Lund. New discoveries were quickly presented to the society in lectures. For example, the young anatomist Carl Magnus Fürst was able to display a reproduction of an X-ray photograph to the society in 1896, the year after Röntgen made his famous discovery. Over half a century later, the professor of diagnostic radiology, Olle Olsson, a scientist with a world-wide reputation, demonstrated the new X-ray television; this was at a lecture in 1959, with the title 'The Revolution in Diagnostic Radiology'. It was thanks to him that Lund became something of an international centre for research and teaching in his subject. As emeritus professor he took part in a new revolution in his field by introducing together with his successor the magnetic resonance tomography technique.

The history of psychiatry can be followed in the society's proceedings: a lecture on the origins and prognosis of paranoia delivered by Bror Gadelius, the lecturer in psychiatry; a lecture in 1931 on 'Psyche and Soma' by Henrik Sjöbring, in which he introduced his psychological theory of types based on 'constitutional radicals'; ten years later he lectured on mild encephalitis as the presumed cause of neuroses. In 1937 Sjöbring's successor as professor of psychiatry, Erik Essen-Möller, delivered a lecture on modern research into twins and what it has demonstrated about the hereditary factors behind schizophrenia; Essen-Möller's later work was done in the field of epidemiological psychiatry, including a work on the registration of familial relations in a rural population.

It was also to the Medical Society in 1921 that the professor of medical chemistry, Erik Widmark, presented his method for determining alcohol levels in the bloodstream. The first cases treated with Thunberg's respirator were presented by the inventor himself in 1926. In 1950 Nils Alwall, later professor of nephrology, gave his views on the treatment of kidney disease, demonstrating techniques and results for treatment with artificial kidneys, a product bearing the Lund trademark which was soon sold world-wide.

A great number of foreign experts in medicine have also addressed the society. Shortly after the end of World War II there came one of the creators of modern antibiotic therapy and winner of a Nobel Prize, Sir Howard Florey, with a lecture on 'The Experimental Background to Clinical Use of Penicillin'. The foreign psychiatrists who have visited the society include N.E. Bleuler from Zurich and Ernst Kretschmer from Tübingen.

Alongside the Medical Society there is another body of medics which deserves mention in a book which occasionally looks at the lighter side of learning in Lund. This is the Medical Association, founded in 1894. The constitution of the association states the joint purpose as lectures and festivities. It is the latter which are better known outside the association, especially the celebration of Toddy Day, always in April. For almost a century now, this example of the odd calendar customs of Lund has involved young medical students dressing up in white coats or rather more imaginative costumes, larking in the streets, and inducing people to buy their humorous — some have said depraved — magazine.

Student life between the wars

The end of the Great War filled the air with a sense of liberation for students in the spring of 1919. On May Eve the Uarda revue played in an atmosphere of gaiety to a packed house; the next day confetti whirled in the May Day breeze. In the following year the carnival was held for the first time in many years, despite those who had claimed that revues and carnivals had disappeared forever from Lund in the grim years of the war.

There were noticeable changes in student life. Before the war was the time of carefree study, commensual companionship, bills of exchange, and eternal students. After the war, study meant more deliberate work towards a professional goal. Refectory fare was scarcely Lucullan, and student credit, although better ordered, was less generous.

In 1922 the student union founded a credit society, the purpose being to offer loans on reasonable terms of interest and repayment. After more than fifty years of successful operation the credit society was closed. By then, from the mid-sixties, there was a government system of study support.

The credit society of 1922 was just one of many new initiatives taken by the students themselves in the years after the First World War. Another was the start of a student newsletter. Earlier attempts had all been ephemeral. Now, following the suggestion of a committee, a student newsletter came into existence, intended as an organ for internal student union affairs. It was also to have space for contributions of a literary, artistic, and social nature. The name chosen for the publication was *Lundagård*, and the first number appeared on 26th March, 1920.

A group of students with literary talent gave *Lundagård* its image during the early 1920s. The playful verse, ironic overtones, and sceptical outlook has often been felt to symbolize what is typically Lundensian. The magazine has retained its role through the decades, and not just as a play-school: many of the editors of the Stockholm press since the 1920s have served their apprenticeship with *Lundagård*.

The greatest change in the social life of the students was the admission of female students. In the 1910s the number of women at the university had risen to 100; in 1930 the figure was over 400. This meant a new life-style; the early complications in the free association of male and female students are documented in numerous novels and poems.

From the twenties on, the female students had attained leading positions in the hitherto male-dominated world of the student union and the nations. The first female chairperson of the student union was elected in 1983. The number of women studying at the university has risen decade by decade, to the extent that many undergraduate courses in the humanities are now numerically dominated by women.

When it comes to obtaining degrees, the female students have been commendably fast (often faster than their male comrades), except where student marriages, cohabitation, household duties, and child-bearing have interfered with the favourable statistics for women. By contrast, the path to the higher academic appointments of lectureships and professorships has proved remarkably slow going for the women. As pointed out earlier, it was not until the inauguration of the new College of Technology in 1965 that Lund could register its first female professor. From the 1980s, however, there have been female professors in all the faculties, except that of theology. A law on the equality of the sexes — justified by the previous under-representation of women in the public sector — is now in force.

The hands on the medieval clock in the cathedral have turned many a revolution since the day late last century when a conservative professor is said to have remarked: 'When I meet a female student in the street, I feel like turning my head away and saying "ugh".' A professor today may also turn his head, but probably in the other direction.

Political currents and echoes of war

After the end of the First World War the frontiers with Europe were opened again. Currency conditions in the countries which had been weakened by war and crisis tempted a new generation to travel, mostly on educational trips, but occasionally on ravaging expeditions.

New ideas were now imported from the south. In 1919 the Frenchman Henri Barbusse, who had served as a soldier at the front, founded a new international association, Clarté. This peace movement, with its fundamentally socialist ideology, sought to tear down the barriers between nations. Three years later a branch of the Clarté association was opened in Lund. It attracted many students with left-wing sympathies, including some from the D.Y.G. group, which was still in existence.

The young Clarté group adopted the ideas of Karl Marx and Sigmund Freud. Marx was not a new name in Lund; his works had been read by left-wing Hegelians back in the 1840s. In the 1930s a new generation of Marxists started the journal *Ateneum*. Their purpose was to make Marx's philosophy of dialectical materialism the foundation of a new science of history and literature. Members of both Clarté and the Ateneum group took a lively part in the debates in the Academic Union.

The chaotic state of Germany after the capitulation and the Versailles Treaty produced different slogans. They were heard and repeated with approval by the young people on the extreme right, who also found inspiration in French intellectual conservatism. In 1924 a national student club was formed as a counter to Clarté. In 1930 a national socialist student association began to hold regular meetings in the Great Hall of the Academic Union.

After Hitler came to power in 1933, the political temperature grew hotter and debates grew more violent. The carnival of 1934 mocked the Third Reich and its jackbooted henchmen. There were still many unsuspecting innocents who would not take the new movement seriously.

The political mood could change from year to year in a student body which was always easily influenced by ideologies. One year the students rejected the proposal that the torchlit procession to the memory of Karl XII be organized under the auspices of the student union; the next year a student referendum rejected the petition of Jewish doctors, refugees from Nazi Germany, to be authorized to practise in Lund.

The question of the Jewish doctors came up in the spring of 1939. In September that year the Second World War broke out. On 30th November, Soviet forces attacked Finland. That year the procession commemorating Karl XII took place without protests; many feared that the Russians would also attack Sweden.

Sympathy for the Finnish cause during the Winter War found expression in collections of money and proclamations of various kinds. Food, clothes, and medicine were sent over the northern border; some students of medicine from Lund volunteered to serve in the medical corps on the front.

The war came geographically closer on 9th April, 1940, when German troops occupied Denmark and Norway. The lights on the other side of the sound were suddenly extinguished, not to come on again for five long years. There was also a blackout in Lund. Conscription decimated the ranks of students and dons.

Academic life was forced to continue in a low key. In April 1940, when a professor of Slavic languages was to be appointed and an expert opinion was called on from Norway, the appointments board received a note from the Swedish Foreign Office, to the effect that no answer could be communicated 'because of the conditions prevailing in Norway.' When the distressing question of a candidate's competence for a lectureship had to be settled by a German expert, the minutes of the meeting recorded that 'Prof. R. Lehmann is at present in a concentration camp in an unknown location.'

On 1st May, 1940, the traditional greeting of the university rector could not take place outside the university building as usual, but within the atrium of the main building; a ban on public meetings was in force. The newly elected rector, the professor of Latin Einar Löfstedt, cited a Roman: 'It is more important to extend the boundaries of the soul than of the empire.'

Political opinion was ambivalent; the old motto of the university — *ad utrumque paratus* 'prepared for both' — has seldom had a more macabre double meaning. The celebration to welcome the newly matriculated students on 4th October, 1940, included a rhetorical address in which Esaias Tegnér, Hegel, and Karl Marx were invoked to defend the course of history as a chain of events controlled by powers which demanded submission. The speaker was an admirer both of the old Germany with its nineteenth-century humanist traditions and — owing to a fatal historico-philosophical confusion — of the new Hitlerite power.

Attitudes like these cannot be dismissed, nor should they be used to prove, as one sometimes hears, that there was a widespread sympathy for Nazism in the university world of Lund. Many of the Nazis' fellow-travellers had gone underground after the German occupation of Denmark and Norway. The Nazi student association, which was still in existence, was stripped of the right to use the premises of the Academic Union in November 1943, following a provocative poster pinned to the union notice-board. Effective anti-Nazi political activity was carried on in associations like the Foreign Politics Club, formed in the thirties, and the Discussion Club, founded in 1942, as well as in other smaller, less official circles.

Following the German occupation of Oslo University in the autumn of 1943, the student union held a protest meeting. The three leading learned societies in Lund, the Physiographic Society, the Society of the Humanities, and the New Society of Letters, passed a joint decision to break off contacts with the official representatives of the Third Reich; German scholars were no longer welcome to lecture before the societies. Three professors, two in the faculty of philosophy, one in the theological faculty, protested against the decision. They declared that they feared grave damage to Swedish academic teaching and research if connections with German scholarship were severed. Their vote, however, was motivated rather by their hope of a German victory.

Important as it is to document such individual expressions of pro-German sympathy, it must also be noted that many undaunted Lundensian and ex-Lundensian voices were heard on Swedish radio and in the press, attacking the ideology and praxis of Nazism. The name of Torgny Segerstedt has already been mentioned. A joint declaration expressing the semi-official attitude of Lund University appeared in *Tidsspegel* in 1942. This publication contained a manifesto signed by representatives of all four faculties, in which they condemned the treachery of the clergy, proclaimed the inviolability of science in a democratic society, and defended freedom of thought and speech against the restrictions which had been imposed.

The occupation of Denmark did not mean that links with Copenhagen University were broken; they were instead intensified. A Nordic student guest committee was formed in 1941; throughout the war significant efforts were made to receive and house students and other refugees.

The situation came to a dramatic head in the autumn of 1943, when the Germans began to persecute Jews in Denmark. The boat-refugees of the period included a group of university teachers, writers, and intellectuals, as well as many students. All of the Copenhagen professors of Jewish birth who passed through or stayed in Lund had previously had contacts with colleagues in Lund University; they included the physicists Niels and Harald Bohr and the philosopher Victor Kuhr. The latter two were asked to teach both Danish and Swedish students at the university, and at the Danish school which had been established to meet the emergency. The Danes formed their own student nation. The sense of community between Lund and Copenhagen was further demonstrated in 1942, when all the professors of Copenhagen University received special diplomatic permission to visit their colleagues in Lund.

From the end of the war to the student revolt

For the academic world in Lund, the days at the end of the war in May 1945 meant the liberation of Denmark and Norway.

The former rector of Oslo University, Didrik Aarup Seip, had been freed from a German concentration camp during the last weeks of the war, thanks to the humanitarian action of the Swedish Red Cross leader, Folke Bernadotte. He was in Lund on 7th May, the day of the German capitulation, when he was spontaneously fêted by a student union procession headed by Norwegian and Danish flags. The same evening he held a memorable speech in the overflowing festival hall of the Academic Union, where practically the entire university was present.

The delayed spring came into full bloom. The sense of liberation after years of suffocating gravity, and the hopes for a new age of peace — soon dashed — overwhelmed young and old alike, even in the peripheral spot on the world map which was Lund, where military action had come no closer than the intruding airborne armadas. The Danish and Norwegian students and their teachers packed their bags and returned from their exile in Lund. The conscripted Swedish students were demobilized. A new epoch began to take shape, with the number of new students that autumn already breaking records and a rapidly expanding teaching staff; the epoch was to bring with it greater changes in the old university than ever before.

Humanitarian and academic contact was resumed at the end of the war with West German universities through the formation of the Münster Committee. The University of Münster, which had suffered heavy bombing during the war, was 'adopted' by Lund. Parcels of food, clothing, and books were dispatched; two thousand students could enjoy Swedish food in public dining-halls.

More significant in the long run were the cultural connections westwards. The Sorbonne opened its doors, as did Oxford and Cambridge. Above all, the road to universities in the United States was opened. All the faculties began an intensive period of scholarly exchange.

In the 1960s Lund University reached an agreement on reciprocal exchange with the University of California and Washington State University in Pullman. Every year some twenty students from California have had visiting scholarships in Lund while a corresponding number of Lund students have studied in the USA. There have since been similar agreements between Lund and far-flung universities in other parts of the world.

A new international consciousness had burgeoned in an academic world which had been isolated for so long by war. One sign of the new broader outlook and the need for increased contact was the start of international courses under the auspices of the student union. In the mid-fifties it was possible to see the flags of thirty-two nations from five continents flying outside the Academic Union. The topics of the courses varied: Co-operative Man; Planning for Tomorrow; The Intellectual and Society; Racism and Nationalism. Interest in the problems of the Third World dominated.

The influx of students from foreign countries to the regular courses offered by the university was such that an International House was built. It came about on the initiative of the Rotary Club, and was opened on 4th May, 1959, by the then Secretary General of the United Nations, Dag Hammarskjöld. The work of the institution came to an end in the wake of the student revolt of 1968 and under pressure of financial difficulties.

The cold war heightened student interest in foreign politics. The crises in Hungary, Czechoslovakia, and Vietnam all led to demonstrations and actions of various kinds. From the mid-sixties there was an increasingly evident politicization and radicalization of the student union or groups within it.

The year of student revolt in Europe, 1968, saw large-scale student unrest also in Lund. Early that year Rudi Dutschke, well-known for his role in the student revolt in Berlin, had been invited to address a student meeting on the subject of 'Studenten und Politik'. During the spring which followed, there were constant reports in the mass media of student protest in various parts of Europe. In nearby Copenhagen there were demonstrations and sit-ins, to slogans like 'Smash the power of the professors!' and 'Co-determination now!' The student union building in Stockholm was occupied. The student revolt reached Lund, partly via remote control.

The powder keg was ignited one late evening in the spring during a symposium on the inflammable theme of 'Science and Politics'. The symposium was a part of the coming anniversary celebrations of the university. Exactly three centuries had passed since Lund University was founded — that too in a time of political uproar. There were preparations for the celebrations of the jubilee with the customary style and pomp. A procession of foreign represen- tatives paraded towards the cathedral in their colourful gowns; those from Lund wore the reintroduced black robes, copied from a model used in the seventeenth century. The invited guests included an academic élite from Europe and the United States, as well as a dozen ambassadors. The distinguished guests were met by a protest organized by a group of radical students, with their three slogans: 'Heath go home! Stop UKAS! Whose is the university?' Heath was the name of the American ambassador. UKAS was the acronym for a government white paper proposing a root-and-branch reorganization of hitherto free university studies. The third slogan called into question not only the existing 'professorial power', but also the authority of those responsible for the form in which the university jubilee was organized.

The police had feared that student riots would break out as they had abroad; the Sorbonne in Paris had been occupied by rebelling students since 12th May, and clouds of tear-gas hung in the air over the Latin Quarter. In Lund, however, there were only isolated incidents, some of which occurred during the stately procession to the cathedral, the central place for the commemoration of this jubilee as for the previous two centennial celebrations. The university rector in 1968 was the professor of surgery, Philip Sandblom, a man with broad horizons and extensive international contacts. In his speech he expressed a message for the day: 'Of all the conceivable ways to resolve a conflict, violence is the worst.'

The jubilee with its festivities and unrest passed, leaving as a permanent memorial a new history of the university. Two volumes appeared in time for the jubilee. The plan for the new history had stated that it would be written as a work of social history, with attention directed towards economic factors, the recruitment of students, and their social conditions. This not only followed a contemporary trend in historical scholarship, but was also in keeping with current discussions concerning the function of the university and its relation to society as a whole in an age of ongoing reform.

The radicalization of the student body — or rather of small groups within it which set the tone for the others — was an accomplished fact in the mid-sixties. The gap widened between the dons, viewed as the bearers of antiquated traditions of knowledge, and a younger generation of critical and militant students. One of the duties of the university, that of communicating knowledge, was now questioned. The word 'critical' became a key concept for the younger generation; it now meant 'critical of society, anticapitalist'.

In 1968 the radical students entrusted a committee with the task of undertaking preparatory work for the opening of an alternative 'critical university'. Marxism played an important role in the debate on theories and methods; voices in several disciplines called for a change of paradigm.

A dramatic sequel to the student revolt of 1968 came the following year at a contact conference between the university and the business world, held in the Academic Union. Students from a group calling themselves Students for a Democratic Society occupied the rostrum and the meeting had to be abandoned. Future protests generally took place at departmental level. In Lund, as elsewhere, the opponents had a stronghold in the department of sociology. After a dramatic election for the position of rector, the annual May Day tribute to the rector was cancelled for the first time in over a century.

After celebrations and counter-celebrations, after the intoxication of revolt and the hangover of disappointment, students returned from protest actions to their workaday routine; the militant element had never been very large. The new government system of study support, in which grants were conditional on the time spent in study and the results achieved, did not permit such extravagant spare-time activities as occupations or year-long protest demonstrations. Ten years after the student revolt the chairman of the student union could observe in a speech: 'The student generation of today plays according to the parliamentary rules which apply to the rest of society.'

In fact, the new generations showed an enthusiasm never witnessed before in their work for reform and their participation in discussions on education policy and the social conditions of students; this was the positive result of the student revolts. New rules on student co-determination have made it possible for students to influence the courses and forms of study during the work of reform which has set its mark on the recent history of the university. In many cases the students have discovered that when it comes to the important questions, they have more in common with their teachers than with the politicians; they form a joint front against the threat of state control from the top, against rigid bureaucracy, and against a closed university.

The negative result of the events of 1968 was a change of attitude on the part of society. The period of university dominance, when large areas of cultural life, pedagogy, and values were still controlled from professorial chairs, and when students were regarded as a privileged élite, was now definitely at an end. The outward face of the university had suffered a considerable loss of prestige. Inside the university the remains of the old élitist professorial power were abolished by administrative reforms. The time of joint decision making had arrived — as long as there was something for dons and students to make joint decisions about other than how to juggle with the resources remaining after financial cutbacks.

Changes in the cultural climate

Ever since the nineteenth century, the most significant new directions and ideas in the various scholarly disciplines at Swedish universities had come from Germany. Practically every scholar of importance in Lund had studied for a time at a German university; this applied equally to theologians, lawyers, natural scientists, medics, and humanists. Men from the first and last of these groups in particular were heavily influenced by a university ideology with its roots in German Romanticism, as proclaimed by scholars like Adolf von Harnack, Ulrich von Wilamowitz-Moellendorff, and Eduard Spranger. Theirs was a cultural philosophy with a strong dash of élitism, critical of tendencies towards mass civilization and Americanization in Europe, and zealous in guarding the role of the university as a cultural and educational focus. Apart from Germany, it was France and England which provided the most fruitful stimuli for the various disciplines.

The twentieth century saw a change in the scholarly climate. The German dominance began to decline after the First World War. Early in the 1930s the deformation of the German universities began, as the traditions of German humanism went up in smoke with the burning books. As someone put it, Hitler closed the European laboratory.

It was only then that the gates were opened wide to admit the flood of culture from the west. Individual scientists and medics from Lund had already found their way to universities in the United States, but from the 1930s the contacts became increasingly intensive. A new era of Anglo-Saxon influence began in the humanities too, with an orientation towards the present and towards methods developed in the behavioural sciences.

A concrete indication of the change in cultural climate can be read in the choice of language used by scholars in Lund. Many were now using English where they had previously written in German for German journals. After the school reforms of the 1940s, the change is evident also in the textbooks used for undergraduate courses; works in German disappear, to be replaced by textbooks in English, often from American presses. American language and culture became a subject of study in Lund with the creation of a lectureship in American English.

The breakaway from a one-sided interest in historical research occurred at roughly the same time in a large number of arts subjects, both linguistic and historical. A symbol of this is the change in the designation of the two disciplines concerned with the study of literature and art, in both of which the suffix *historia* was replaced by *vetenskap* 'science'. It is not just the name which has changed: research too has diverted its interest towards the twentieth century, contemporary phenomena, and a synchronic perspective. A new chair of art was created, specializing in the role and function of art in modern society.

The bias towards the present day and the social orientation go hand in hand. The establishment of a faculty of social sciences in 1946 was a declaration of independence for a group of new disciplines, among them economic history and sociology.

Influences from the social and behavioural sciences have affected many subjects in all the faculties. In theology, where historical and linguistic interests now took a back seat, a new professorship has been created for the psychology and sociology of religion. In the faculty of law there are now chairs of employment law and sociology of law. The medical faculty has professors of social medicine and occupational medicine, and there is even a subject with the bold name of social odontology. The tendency in all these cases is evident: to gear research and teaching to the direct service of contemporary social development. The statement of a 1947 committee on the social sciences is typical in this respect: all research in the social sciences is there said to be intended 'as a stage in the process which will lead to the realization of the principles of popular government.' The attainment of a democratic society thereby becomes the ultimate goal of all scientific research in Sweden. Not since the Age of Freedom has the purpose of the university been so directly linked to contemporary social utility.

One of the general changes in the scientific climate of the post-war period is the direction of research away from the individual. This applies first and foremost to the objects of research. Systems, classes, and groups have increasingly become fields of research in disciplines like history, literature, and art, while scholars of previous generations preferred to study the work of individual politicians, authors, or artists.

Research has become less centred on individuals in yet another respect. In the modern university world the lone scholar working in private has been to a certain extent replaced by the collective project. Teams of researchers were active first in laboratory and experimental subjects, in science and medicine, but now the humanities have also seen the establishment of groups of research students under a single supervisor and research projects, often financed by the research councils.

Another far-reaching tendency is, as we have seen, the differentiation into increasingly specialized subjects. This has been a necessary precondition for development in science and medicine, as also in the humanities. Yet specialization has also led at times to isolation within narrow fields of scholarship. To counter this we now have interdisciplinary studies, which have had their most successful practical applications in science, technology, and medicine.

There is today a world-wide demand for the holistic approach which considers the interplay of man and nature as a whole. Our age of specialization has witnessed the revival of the romantic dream of a total view, a new *universitas scientiarum*, although hitherto this has been more of a utopia than a reality.

Expansion and crisis

In the critical tricentennial year of 1968, Lund University had 14,000 students. A century previously the number had been a modest 350. The idyllic small-town academy where everyone knew everyone else had become a university on the same scale as its larger European counterparts, with an annual budget of around 700,000,000 kronor, twenty years later almost twice this sum. The expansion is a reflection of changes in society at large, with its growing population and the increasing need for labour with academic qualifications.

The growth of the student body did not proceed gradually, but by leaps and bounds. The periods of expansion have followed fluctuations in the economy, mostly coming in conjunction with periods of decline. Up to 1909 the number of students never exceeded 1,000. In the mid-twenties it rose just above the 2,000 mark; at the start of the 1950s it was 3,000. Only after that did the curve rise rapidly. At the end of the sixties the number was around 15,000; in later decades it has reached 20,000 in a town of 80,000 inhabitants (including over 4,000 immigrants).

In 1870, when Sweden was still overwhelmingly an agrarian country, 31 per cent of the students came from farming families. This proportion fell steadily during the next century, levelling off around 9 per cent in the 1940s and 1950s. At the start of the period as many as 13 per cent were sons of clergy, but only 4 per cent came from this background at the end. The proportion of children of academics rose from 8 per cent to 12 per cent (in direct figures from 9 individuals to 215). The number of students from professional homes likewise increased steadily, from 8 per cent to 18 per cent. The most striking statistic shows that recruitment from working-class homes was low over the entire period, although it did increase from 8 to 12 per cent (in real numbers from 9 individuals in 1870 to 214 a century later). In this respect the changes do not correspond to social development as a whole. To express it bluntly, Lund University has had and continues to have a solidly middle-class character, reflecting the view of culture which was also typical of other universities in Europe until the Second World War. The symbolic world of university education, its entire semiotic system, is largely designed to suit the ideology of the middle class, to which in its turn it helps to give its form.

The greatest expansion from the 1940s and 1950s was in the faculty of philosophy, where teaching was not narrowly geared to future occupations. It was to this faculty that the increasing number of female students applied. Modern languages and the aesthetic subjects became popular. In the 1930s, in an earlier period of economic crisis, the number of graduates from the faculty had already exceeded the needs of the labour market. In the 1950s and later, however, when the hordes of young people caused an educational explosion, the university was faced with new problems, concerning the university both as a study environment and as a research centre.

A government commission was set up in 1955 with the primary task of improving the slow pace of study and the high drop-out rate which had resulted from the growth of the philosophy faculty. Cold figures showed that 40 per cent of arts students left the university without having taken a degree.

The old forms of study were dominated by professorial lectures and seminars, with long periods between examinations. The new commission proposed a form of teaching closer to that used in schools. Teaching at undergraduate level required a new category of lecturer, the *lektor*, whose work was concentrated on shorter courses involving more regular testing. No class was to exceed thirty students; as new courses were established, new lecturers were to be appointed. This automatic mechanism was expected to preserve a free sector at the university, avoiding the necessity for the minimum school grades required by the medical faculty.

The proposal of the commission was approved by parliament in 1958. The number of the new category of lecturers rose rapidly. In the mid-sixties there were (including ordinary, extraordinary, and acting lecturers) over ninety in the faculties concerned. The ordinary lecturers had a seat on the faculty boards, and in most cases also a vote; this meant a shift in the majority in what had once been assemblies of professors.

As so often in the dialectic of history, the quantitative change with the rapid increase in the number of students led to a qualitative shift. The demand for a faster 'throughput' — one of the keywords of the debate on education in the 1950s and 1960s — led to a reduction in the standards required for the old examinations. The examinations statute from the beginning of the century was abolished and replaced by a regulation with tougher control of studies.

It was this reform, known as UKAS or PUKAS, which was so hotly debated. After it was passed in 1969, studies in the faculty of philosophy were incorporated into a number of different course programmes (Swedish *utbild-ningslinjer* ('education lines'), each adapted to the expected needs of the labour market. Syllabuses for all the country's universities were drawn up, catalogued, and timetabled. The old graded degrees disappeared, to be replaced by a system of study points or credits; one year's study was to represent 40 points (20 points for each of the two terms of the academic year), and 120 points would thus correspond to the former degree.

Postgraduate studies were also restructured. Doctors were no longer to receive degrees, instead qualifying with a 'doctor's examination' with a dissertation of limited format. Each doctoral student was to have an officially appointed supervisor. A four-year postgraduate research grant was introduced, to be replaced in 1984 by doctoral studentships involving a certain amount of teaching duties. The external forms of the doctoral examination were simplified: the disputation itself was made less dramatic and more democratic. Graded qualifications were abolished; the wearing of tails at the disputation ceased, and the institution of the second and third opponent in most cases disappeared.

The examination system in all the faculties was circumscribed. The 1970s saw a definitive — thus far — transformation of what had once been 'free' studies. The austere climate of the national economy has brought about a freeze in university education across the board: the intake of students is supposed to correspond to the demand of the labour market. The number of people applying for admission each year still greatly exceeds what the university with its limited resources can accept. Admission depends in the first instance on high-school grades. Work experience has also counted as a qualification, a factor which has somewhat raised the average age of the students.

The latest reform of the 1980s has left the university with only two categories of teacher — professor and lecturer (*högskolelektor*) — as well as two-year appointments as research assistant. The pursuit of a traditional research career has been hampered by the disappearance of the position of *docent*. The reform cannot guarantee reasonable opportunities for research and for the graduates who have the talent to undertake it.

The nineteenth-century dream of the university as an independent centre of learning has been transformed by the latest reforms into an institute where everything is regulated within a rigid social framework. Under the older regime, undergraduate studies were organized largely according to the ultimate goals of scholarship. In the new educational institute, undergraduate studies have become a goal in themselves, resulting in a widened gap between graduate and postgraduate studies. In the old days students 'went up' to university; now they attend courses. It is not just the increased volume of knowledge which has caused the fragmentation; it is also the lack of a unifying university ideology.

The institutional organization of Lund University had been relatively unchanged between the 1870s and the Second World War. It was based on the classic four faculties. In a few decades, however, from the 1950s to the 1980s, the organization of the university has experienced a greater revolution than during the previous three centuries. The first change was the erection of the two sections of the philosophy faculty into two separate faculties, one of arts, one of mathematics and natural sciences. A new faculty was created for economics in 1961. Three years later a faculty of social sciences was broken out of the arts faculty; economics was then incorporated into the new social science faculty. In 1954 an odontological faculty arose when the College of Dentistry in Malmö was incorporated into the university. Lund College of Technology, inaugurated in 1965, was incorporated into the university after a short period of independence. The four original faculties, with their roots in the medieval structure of the Sorbonne in Paris, have thus become eight.

The aim of the reforms of the 1950s and 1960s has been to tie the university and its structure to contemporary society and its social, economic, and cultural structure. After the latest reform of tertiary education in 1977, the faculties are no longer independent corporations except on paper. Their function has been taken over by other bodies, faculty boards, study programme committees, appointments boards; all the boards have representatives not only from the teaching staff but also from the student body and the technical and administrative personnel. The university board, which has replaced the Consistory, has a similar composition, with representatives also from the professions and 'society at large'. Gone forever is the old hierarchical structure of the university, based on the organization of the medieval monasteries and guilds.

The relative sizes of the various faculties reveal an obvious shift in the centre of gravity away from the arts towards the social sciences, medicine, science, and engineering. This reflects the technical and bureaucratic revolution which has transformed Sweden from the agrarian society of the nineteenth century to today's industrial state.

For a long time now the smallest faculty has been the one which was once first in size and rank: theology. The arts faculty has also developed at a modest pace. Since the social scientists left to become autonomous, the number of professorial chairs in the two sections, history-philosophy and languages, remained at twenty-four for a long time.

Research potential in science and medicine has increased much more quickly, accelerating during and after the Second World War. In 1980 the faculty of technology had sixty professors. In the same year the science faculty with its three sections had thirty-seven professors. Apart from ordinary professorships there are a number of research appointments at various levels, the costs of which are financed by research councils or the university, and to a great extent also by funds and grants from private industry. It is rare for the humanities to benefit from private grants — a striking exception is the recent donation of a chair of book and library history by a noted publisher and bibliophile.

Equally telling are the figures which illustrate the growth of the faculty of medicine. In 1868 the faculty consisted of only three professors and three assistant lecturers, which had grown by 1930 to the modest total of fourteen professors and one assistant lecturer; by 1968, however, the teaching staff consisted of 48 professors, 16 associate professors, and a further 356 teachers ranging from senior physicians to teaching assistants are listed in the university catalogue.

Concrete evidence of the growth of the university can be seen in the way the face of the town has changed. A general plan was drawn up in 1948, with proposals for the physical expansion of the university and its departments. A modern hospital was built north of the university area and the former hospital clinics in the course of the 1950s and 1960s. This reflects not only the development and differentiation of medical science but also society's demands for health service facilities. The hospital could take a maximum of 36 patients when it was established in the 1780s, 5,000 patients at the start of this century, and 30,000 patients annually in the 1970s. The new Central Block, designed by an immigrant architect, Stephan Hornyánszky, was completed in 1968. Since then the contour of Lund from a distance does not consist of the poet's 'silver-grey towers' but the blue-grey block; two large parabolic aerials have been placed on the roof of the hospital block. This can be interpreted as one of many symbols of the secularization which has transformed the university town, where *sapientia divina* has given way to *sapientia humana*.

The redbrick buildings of the College of Technology are grouped together to the north. They make up a new faculty village, built close to the university's science departments. The architect Klas Anshelm designed in modern functional style no less than six of the buildings for the College of Technology, as well as most of the arts departments at Helgonabacken.

When the hospital moved north, the university took over the southern area of the hospital as planned; the old buildings now house administration, law, social sciences, and some arts subjects. At the moment of writing, a white-haired emeritus professor is sitting bent over a typewriter in a room in one of these buildings, engaged in composing what one Lund poet has called 'our stanza in the long poem about a town'.

A town and a university which have been constantly reshaped over the years. Of the university which had its forms and functions determined three hundred years ago, the latest organizational reforms have left little, hardly even the name. According to the organization which has been in force since 1st July, 1977, the *högskola* 'college of higher education' in Lund, which the state authorities generously allow to retain the name of Lund University, is now a part of one of the country's six higher education planning regions, the Lund/Malmö Higher Education Planning Region. Each region has — at least at present — a regional board with the duty of co-ordinating all tertiary education within the region.

Apart from the university with its eight faculties, the Lund/Malmö Higher Education Planning Region comprises a number of previously independent institutes of higher education, divided into five administrative areas.

The basic units in the administration of the university are the individual departments. At the head of each department is a *prefekt*, who is also chairman of the departmental board.

The huge and multivarious university has undoubtedly become what one university rector has termed 'Sweden's largest bank of knowledge'. In the mid-1980s Lund University had 22,000 students in some fifty different study programmes. There are about 2,500 active research students in the eight faculties. Yet individual units within the university which has grown to this size have already been threatened by subdivision or closure. Anyone who wants to view a complex situation optimistically can observe that research and teaching have managed to survive every university reform hitherto, and will probably survive the latest too.

The main duty of the university has been encroached upon by the administrative work included in teaching and research appointments. Another threat is, paradoxically enough, the invasion of professional bureaucrats. Right up to the beginning of World War II, the local administration of the university was managed by a handful of officials. The great university reforms meant a growth in both the number and the responsibilities of the bureaucrats. Even at a time when the number of students and teachers has been reduced, some Parkinsonian law has allowed the central administration to swell. The years 1974–81 have seen an estimated increase of 41 per cent in the central administration.

The crisis in the modern university world is an international phenomenon, which can only in part be blamed on the expansion of bureaucracy. In a harsh economic climate the university is forced to make cuts, to reduce the number of people employed (although this happens mostly on the research and teaching side), to decrease study support, to cut financial allowances for the purchase of books and equipment by the departments. Research and teaching are assessed according to narrow economic criteria based on those applied in private industry, like the production of profitable and unprofitable merchandise.

It is on the humanities side that the university has been particularly hard hit. Humanistic study in the mid-eighties is financed to considerably more than half — almost 80 per cent in fact — by a government grant. The corresponding figure for science and medicine is around 50 per cent. This means that a much greater proportion of external funds has been made available for medical and scientific research: private donations have mostly favoured medicine; when industry commissions research it is mainly in science and engineering. The present importance of external funding for the university economy — in Sweden as elsewhere — involves the risk that concentration on short-term goals may lead to a neglect of the basic research which is the essence of scholarship.

Yet the crisis in the university is also internal. It is connected with the gigantic explosion of knowledge which has made it difficult to obtain a structured overview of the extent to which knowledge has grown. Specialization has led to a feeling of estrangement between different disciplines, an inability to understand the concepts and values of scholars in other subjects. The rapid succession of trends and fashions in method and theory may also have contributed to the instability of the intellectual milieu, perhaps in the humanities in particular. The criteria for what is accepted as good or bad research are not as self-evident as they once were, and even the concept of 'scholarship' — once a watchword — has in some academic circles taken on negative connotations.

189

It is a fact that since 1968 the university reforms have had an anti-academic tendency, which has contributed to the demolishing of what was once a more homogeneous intellectual environment. At the same time as the academic requirements for admission have been reduced and the élitist features of university life have been abolished, there has come stricter adherence to regulations and greater segmentation, which can hardly have helped to further independent and creative work.

It must be admitted that a university which is regulated in every detail, technicalized, computerized, and thoroughly bureaucratized, would be a conceivable reflection of Swedish society today. Yet the goal of a university can never be merely to reproduce an existing society. It must also have a cultural function. The humanities in the new university have found it increasingly difficult to justify their existence. They do not contribute to technical development or economic growth. Their purpose is to interpret and explain man's role as a cultural being; only the liberal arts can define the values by which we live; they alone can provide alternatives and utopias for a life of greater humanity, far beyond the walls of the university.

Reduced standards and restricted goals threaten the traditional duties of the university as they have been formed and performed over the years. One of these central duties is the creation of an environment favourable to the passing on and renewal of knowledge, a seedbed for creativity and criticism, with the purpose of rediscovering and reinterpreting the past, illuminating the present, and conquering the future.

Inbetween sky and the sea, the plains and the sloping down,
like wind-blown leaf on a roof, is the site of our town.
Perchance, 'tis the wind, for some hundreds of years making fast,
until ready to hurl it onto the straits at last.

Göran Printz-Påhlson

Epilogue
Lund and Europe
The quintessential Lund

In the centrally controlled state of Sweden, Lund is at a distance of 400 miles from the capital, the seat of government and administration. The town is in a peripheral location with respect to the centres of power. At the same time, Lund is closer to a foreign capital and university — Copenhagen — than any other Swedish university.

Two factors in particular have determined the special character of the environment and atmosphere of Lund University from the seventeenth century to the twentieth: the provincial and the continental. The provincial, noticeably Southern Swedish touch comes from the geographical location, the climate, and the dialect. Many of the families whose names recur over the centuries in the history of the university had their roots in the local landscape. The southern accent with its uvular *r* and its diphthongs has been spoken by students and professors alike, while the folk-speech of the province has been studied by dialectologists and collected by the Dialect and Place-Name Archive.

It is perhaps surprising to see the extent to which the geographical situation has influenced the topics of research in both science and arts disciplines. It was in the mild climate of Southern Sweden that Erik Gustaf Lidbeck, professor of natural history and director of the Scanian plantations, was bold and hopeful enough to plant mulberry trees on a scale sufficient to initiate silk production in the eighteenth century. A long series of Lund botanists — Elias Fries, Fredrik Areschough, Henning Weimarck — have each written a *Flora Scanica* following excursions into the local botanical terrain. When the Lund Botanical Association was formed in 1858, the first expedition went to Lund Cathedral; in the joints between the sandstone blocks there grew (and still grows) a rare type of wall-rue, *Asplenium ruta muraria*, a little green fern, along with some forty other plant species. It is natural that the genus *Salix* should have been an object of study in a province distinctive for its hedges of pollarded willow, and that several generations of Lund botanists should have studied the genus *Rubus* which grows abundantly in Southern Sweden. The experiments in crossing seed types carried out by Nilsson-Ehle, Arne Münzing, and their successors were well suited to the soil of Scania. It is hardly surprising that the geologists of Lund have examined rocks and mineral finds from the south of Sweden. On the other hand, the provincial ties must not be exaggerated. A domicile in Lund has not prevented geologists, botanists, and zoologists from undertaking research expeditions to study Arctic regions, coral islands in the Pacific, algae in the Mediterranean, or the animal life of Africa and America.

Observations concerning the way Lund scholars have concentrated on their own province can be extended to a number of arts subjects as well. This applies to historians and archaeologists. Unique documents in the University Library like *Liber Daticus* and *Necrologium Lundense*, together with medieval manuscripts from Scania preserved in the Royal Library in Copenhagen, have attracted generations of historians to explore the Danish period in the history of the province and the town. Nordic archaeologists have found inexhaustible material for study in the Scanian soil and the medieval churches — above all Lund Cathedral. Ecclesiastical historians have found the plentiful local sources a fruitful basis for the study of the bishops, the revival movements, and the church customs of the Diocese of Lund.

Another example comes from the Folklife Archive, which was given official status in 1913. The recorders of folk tradition obviously concentrated their efforts on the south of Sweden. Carl Wilhelm von Sydow, professor of Scandinavian and comparative folklife studies in Lund, was a pupil of the Danish specialist in folk poetry, Axel Olrik. Sydow's research into Celtic features in Germanic poetry, sagas, and folktales reflects the comparative method which was typical of international scholarship at that time. Much of his material on popular tales and traditions came from the treasury of lore collected in the provinces of Southern Sweden. This material included the tale of the Finn, who has been associated in local tradition with the building of Lund Cathedral and a sculpture in the crypt known as 'Finn the Giant'. The saga of Finn has also interested literary writers, from Esaias Tegnér to James Joyce. In *Finnegans Wake* Joyce tells in his idiosyncratic English that Finn 'built the Lund's kirk and destroyed the church's land; who guess his title grabs his deed.'

Modern folklife studies, now with the more up-to-date designation of ethnology, has diversified its interests. Alongside the old peasant culture, the subject now includes the study of urban and industrial cultural forms and everyday life.

The profile of the university over the years has thus undeniably reflected its deep provincial roots and its geographical catchment area. In recent times these close regional ties have been reinforced by the changes in education policy which have made Lund the headquarters for all institutions of higher education in the towns of Southern Sweden. Regional affinity has been further strengthened since the 1980s by the ever closer contact with commerce and industry in Southern Sweden, as displayed in the Ideon project.

If the provincial is one important side of university life, the other, no less

The crypt of Lund Cathedral, where the high altar was consecrated in 1123. Tombstones of church dignitaries and Scanian noblemen are set in the floor. On one pillar is a carving of the legendary giant Finn.

important, is the continental. From the very first days of the university a network of contacts has been developed via a two-way channel of communication. Scholarly ideals and methodologies have been borrowed from the great cultural centres of Europe, quickly transmitted by virtue of the geographical and cultural proximity to the continent.

Foreign studies were a part of the normal educational career of university teachers right from the first decades of the Caroline Academy. Foreign connections began to decline in the Age of Freedom and the Gustavian epoch, but the nineteenth century saw renewed and extended contacts with continental universities; this was the era of educational tours (often lasting several years) and scientific congresses.

The road to the continental world of learning often went via Copenhagen. Right from the seventeenth century, professors had travelled over the sound to meet colleagues and to acquire the scholarly literature which had not yet reached Sweden. In 1830 Carl Adolph Agardh wrote in *Lunds Weckoblad* of the place of the university on the map: 'Lund University has (with respect to ease of communication) one of the most splendid positions in Sweden. Only a few hours are needed to transport oneself at a trifling cost to the capital of another kingdom, which has the largest libraries, institutes, and collections in Scandinavia, and at the same time to an assembly of littérateurs who distinguish themselves as much by their genuine learning as by their true humanity.' The proximity to Copenhagen eased the problems of obtaining foreign books, journals, and newspapers. From another note by Agardh we know that it did not take him more than a fortnight to have a book sent from Leipzig to Lund. The University Library was the first in the country to commence regular exchanges of scholarly literature with foreign libraries; the year was 1818. It was in 1826 that C.W.K. Gleerup came from Copenhagen to Lund to found the bookshop which was soon to become the university bookshop. He was the first to attempt to disseminate foreign literature on any scale in Sweden; he also helped to make Swedish literature known abroad, both as a bookseller and as a publisher.

Edvard Lehmann, the Dane who came from Berlin in the 1910s to become professor of the history of religion, coined the proverbial description of Lund as 'the threshold to Europe'. Copenhagen was the door.

Many people took the step over the threshold. From the mid-nineteenth century the travelling time was reduced by the railway and the steamboats. For generations of Lund students the continent was closer than it was for their contemporaries in Uppsala. Many writers have testified to this, among them Bertil Malmberg:

> For it is undeniable: the pre-war spring was redolent of Europe. ... When the temperate spring breeze blew down Klostergatan and across Mårtenstorget, and Lundagård came into leaf, then every normal student felt an awakening desire for travel and pleasure. It was then, as now, a varied range of wishes and dreams which followed the passage of the clouds over the roofs, or the wisps of smoke through the open windows of the studies. Some of these wishes and dreams concerned bodily things, beer tankards and female hips, fairground losses and pavement cafés, some concerned art museums and libraries, some theatres, some meetings with famous men, some nothing more than fleeting days in city streets.

Lund's location has made it something of an intellectual meeting place. Communications have been open in both directions. A small élite of European scholars have found their way here. New communications, however, have brought about a change for the worse in Lund's location. In the days of the railway it was a natural stop-off for visiting lecturers on their way north, whether to Stockholm or Uppsala. In the age of the aeroplane, however, the town risks being literally and figuratively overlooked. Yet tradition still dictates that the winners of the Nobel Prizes for science each year deliver lectures in Lund. Since the end of the Second World War the town has also found a place on the intellectual map as a congress centre.

Every new student generation in a university which nevertheless still lies on the fringe of Europe has benefited from the transmission of influences from Europe and the USA by the foreign lectors. After working as ambassadors for the language and culture of their respective countries, many of them have returned home — as professors of Scandinavian studies. Some examples may illustrate this two-way process of communication. Mario Gabrieli, Italian lector in Lund in the 1940s and 1950s, later became professor of Scandinavian languages in Naples. Otto Oberholzer from Switzerland, a specialist in the writings of Pär Lagerkvist, returned from Lund to become professor of Scandinavian studies in Kiel, where he initiated a project on the links between Germany and Scandinavia. One of his predecessors as German lector, Ernst Alker, finished his career as professor of German literature in Fribourg; he wrote the articles on Swedish culture and literature in *Der grosse Brockhaus* and published essays on Ibsen, Sigrid Undset, Johannes Edfelt, and other Scandinavian authors.

One of the legendary foreign lectors in the 1930s was Arthur H. King, who brought with him from his student days in Cambridge a new wave of English culture: he lectured on Joyce and T.S. Eliot, on I.A. Richards and William Empson. He took his doctorate in Lund (supervised by Ekwall) with a dissertation on the language of English Renaissance drama. One of his pupils wrote: 'This extraordinary man had a capacity to enliven the written word, whereby he enriched both the emotional and intellectual life of his students for the rest of their lives.' The same distinguished group of lectors in the 1920s and 1930s included Paul Tisseau, a man with a schooling in French philosophy. During his years as lector in Lund he translated into French a number of Søren Kierkegaard's works, thus preparing the way for French existentialism. It should be added that lectors in Danish, Norwegian, and Finnish, on return to their homelands, have often ended up as professors or editors in Copenhagen, Oslo, Bergen, and Helsinki.

In many important respects the international cultural situation has changed: the poles are no longer Lund and Europe. A commission on the internationalization of Swedish universities in the 1970s saw it as its most urgent task to broaden the perspective towards a world beyond Europe and America, towards

Asia, Africa, and the developing nations in general. Such a broadened perspective has also come about, although limited in scope, partly through the immigrant students and visiting students, partly through changes in the content of the old university subjects. Concrete examples are the new subjects of Middle Eastern studies and North African studies, with their multi- and interdisciplinary approach; the arts, theology, and social sciences meet science, technology, and medicine in a blend which is in demand for the development work going on in the Middle East and North Africa.

At the same time, the international outlook has narrowed irreparably in other respects. The potential ability to survey foreign literature — whether scientific or artistic — which knowledge of the three main European languages allowed a generation ago, is no longer there for the new generation of students who have been victims of the reduced language teaching resulting from Swedish educational policy. This is another palpable cultural loss. The shrinking of both linguistic and temporal horizons is evident from a decade-by-decade comparison of requirements for various university subjects. The same can be observed from a glance at the bibliographies of literature referred to in doctoral dissertations.

It is customary — and perhaps best — to characterize universities in contrasting pairs: Cambridge and Oxford, Heidelberg and Jena, Lund and Uppsala.

For centuries Lund lived in the shadow of the older, royal university in Uppsala, and only gradually established its own special character through contrasts and cautious competition. At the start of the nineteenth century Carl Adolph Agardh attempted to define the difference between the two universities thus: 'Uppsala is the upper chamber, with its brilliant ancestry, living in ideas; Lund is the lower chamber, healthily unpretentious by virtue of its realistic outlook.'

Uppsala, with its Vasa Castle and its monumental buildings from the days of Olof Rudbeck and Carl von Linnaeus, makes a more magnificent impression as a town. Lund's more modest style can even be observed in the memorials to departed scholars in the cemeteries. The professorial authoritarianism in Uppsala, which can be seen in a stronger tendency towards the formation of schools, has probably been less typical of the academic atmosphere in Lund. The more democratic character of social and academic life in the southern university town is something which memoir writers and other observers have claimed to be able to discern for over two hundred years. In the days when parliament represented the old estates, the percentage of students from the nobility was always higher in Uppsala than in Lund; when royal princes have undertaken university studies, they have always chosen Uppsala. Throughout the nineteenth century most of the leading politicians and higher secular state officials came from Uppsala. By contrast, some leading twentieth-century politicians and ministers in Social Democratic governments have come from Lund.

From the point of view of climate, there is a great difference between the two towns; Uppsala has longer and harsher winters, a more arctic climate. Lund has, according to meteorological criteria, the longest spring of any town in Sweden. One Scanian poet with associations with Lund has felt justified in describing winter in the province as a 'secret spring'; the prevailing weather may also have influenced the spiritual climate.

Comparisons of Lund with other European universities are more hazardous, but may nevertheless be revealing. Lund shares with Cambridge something of the impudent spirit which the latter university displays in its well-known *Varsity Handbook*. Lund shows a similar lack of respect in its carnivals, when every four years the university abandons method for madness; each new generation demonstrates its irreverence for all authority and satirizes the age and the world in which it lives, including the academic environment. Moreover, the Footlights revues in Cambridge, where many illustrious comic talents have served their apprenticeship, have a direct counterpart in the Lundensian *spex*. A more serious comparison of Lund with the town on the Cam would look at the development of the research village of Ideon, which has been modelled on British science parks, chiefly those in Cambridge and Edinburgh.

From the very beginning the German universities provided Lund — as Uppsala before it — with a model for its organization. The traditions of German student life have scarcely any reflections in Lund other than borrowings from the treasury of student songs. 'O, alte Burschenherrlichkeit' has been sung at the feasts of the student nations well into the present century in its Swedish version, 'O gamla klang- och jubeltid'; another tune which is traditionally played at the opening of all the *spex* revues on the last day of April is 'Jung muss man sein'. Finally, there may be at bottom a certain affinity between the mentality which has earned the name of *der Heidelberger Geist* — with its ironical distance to bourgeois philistinism, its cerebral spirituality, and its élitism — and the *Lundaskepticism* which had its most typical representatives in the inter-war years.

Yet if the concept of Lund and the Lundensian has retained anything of its significance over the centuries, this has only been possible through the continuity of the transformation process. The truth is that each new generation has both moulded and been moulded by the specific atmosphere of the university town.

One eccentricity which Lund indubitably shares with all university towns is that it never really grows old. The population structure distinguishes it from other towns of the same size: it is rejuvenated with every transient student generation. For the majority of students Lund is merely a place to pass through, a station on their journey through life. Only a few students in each generation linger here: as perpetual students, as lecturers, as professors — the boundaries between the different categories are fluid.

As a town of youth, Lund is a place of expectations and disappointments. Each new generation feels this in various aspects of life, including the intellectual. During the three centuries which have elapsed, Lund has not always been able to quench the youthful thirst for knowledge and discovery. At the beginning of the 1780s the professor of history Sven Lagerbring wrote in a letter: 'With us everything is, as usual, in its constant state of stagnation.' This lamentation is repeated time and again. More than one Lundensian scholar, having taken a doctorate here only to be ejected by the academic machinery, has depicted the research community as backward Abderites.

No attempt will be made here to draw up a final balance sheet for Lund University. Instead, the last word will be given to a Lundensian who saw from a distance the town where he had spent his youthful years. Torgny Segerstedt had undeniably been the victim of maltreatment in the intrigues about academic appointments, and was thus forced to pursue his career outside the university. Yet his heart was still in Lund.

Torgny Segerstedt's words about Lund appeared in the Gothenburg newspaper of which he was editor, *Göteborgs Handels och Sjöfartstidning*. The article was written in connection with the 250th anniversary celebrations of the university in 1918. It is at once a historical and a personal view, tinged with a nostalgia which has been accentuated with the years:

Research always has the forward-seeking drive of the youthful pathfinder. It brings the latest ideas of the times to minds still fresh and receptive, where they will find a foothold and a lair. Study and research preserve life's youthful lustre, while their bearers pass by one after the other. One by one they have been carried into the ancient cathedral, student songs have resounded under the heavy arches, and the white standard has been lowered in a final farewell out in one of the bowery graveyards. Research and youth have lived on, young as ever.

One generation comes and another goes. Nothing remarkable has happened, everything is and will remain as it has been. Only he who has gone has changed a trifle from the day when he first with pounding heart sets foot on the soil of Lundagård, until the bright spring evening when he makes the final rounds of the lecture halls and faculty rooms of the university, standing before the portraits of departed scholars which adorn the walls. It is this long succession of researchers whose quiet toil has borne along a piece of Swedish culture. Most of them slumber in the oblivion of their graves. Many names have been forgotten, their features never immortalized on canvas. A few live in the annals of scholarship. Yet it feels as if an invisible bond ties one to them all. They have all made their contribution to the spirit which characterizes work at the Southern Swedish university, all have created the tradition which sets its stamp on the sons [and now also daughters] of Alma Mater Carolina.

Literature

Bibliographical note complementary to the bibliography in the Swedish edition.

Bourdieu, Pierre. *Homo academicus*. Paris 1984.

Classen P., Wolgast E. *Kleine Geschichte der Universität Heidelberg*. Berlin, Heidelberg, New York 1983.

Elias, Norbert. *Über den Prozess der Zivilisation* 1–2. 1978. Frankfurt am Main 5 Aufl. 1978.

d'Irsay Stephen. *Histoire des universités françaises et étrangères*. 1–2. Paris 1933–1935.

Niléhn, Lars. *Peregrinatio academica*. Lund 1983.

Ringer, Fritz. *Education and Society in modern Europe*. Blommington 1979.

— *The decline of the German mandarine*. Massachusets 1967.

Samuel von Pufendorf 1632–1982. *Ett rättshistoriskt symposium i Lund 1982*. Lund 1986.

Index of names cited